ULYSSES S. GRANT

ULYSSES S. GRANT

A Biography

Robert P. Broadwater

GREENWOOD BIOGRAPHIES

 GREENWOOD

AN IMPRINT OF ABC-CLIO, LLC
Santa Barbara, California • Denver, Colorado • Oxford, England

Copyright 2012 by ABC-CLIO, LLC

Library of Congress Cataloging-in-Publication Data

Broadwater, Robert P., 1958–
  Ulysses S. Grant : a biography / Robert P. Broadwater.
    p. cm. — (Greenwood biographies)
  Includes index.
  ISBN 978-0-313-39255-9 (hardback) — ISBN 978-0-313-39256-6 (ebook)
1. Grant, Ulysses S. (Ulysses Simpson), 1822–1885.   2. Generals—United States—Biography.   3. United States. Army—Biography.   4. United States—History—Civil War, 1861–1865—Biography.   I. Title.
  E672.B864   2012
  973.8'2092—dc23
  [B]   2011050444

ISBN: 978-0-313-39255-9
EISBN: 978-0-313-39256-6

16 15 14 13 12   1 2 3 4 5

This book is also available on the World Wide Web as an eBook.
Visit www.abc-clio.com for details.

Greenwood
An Imprint of ABC-CLIO, LLC

ABC-CLIO, LLC
130 Cremona Drive, P.O. Box 1911
Santa Barbara, California 93116-1911

This book is printed on acid-free paper ∞

Manufactured in the United States of America

CONTENTS

CONTENTS

SERIES FOREWORD

In response to school and library needs, ABC-CLIO publishes this distinguished series of full-length biographies specifically for student use. Prepared by field experts and professionals, these engaging biographies are tailored for students who need challenging yet accessible biographies. Ideal for school assignments and student research, the length, format, and subject areas are designed to meet educators' requirements and students' interests.

ABC-CLIO offers an extensive selection of biographies spanning all curriculum-related subject areas including social studies, the sciences, literature and the arts, history and politics, and popular culture, covering public figures and famous personalities from all time periods and backgrounds, both historic and contemporary, who have made an impact on American and/or world culture. The subjects of these biographies were chosen based on comprehensive feedback from librarians and educators. Consideration was given to both curriculum relevance and inherent interest. Readers will find a wide array of subject choices from fascinating entertainers like Miley Cyrus and Lady Gaga to inspiring leaders like John F. Kennedy and Nelson Mandela, from the greatest athletes of our time like Michael Jordan and Lance

Armstrong to the most amazing success stories of our day like J. K. Rowling and Oprah.

While the emphasis is on fact, not glorification, the books are meant to be fun to read. Each volume provides in-depth information about the subject's life from birth through childhood, the teen years, and adulthood. A thorough account relates family background and education, traces personal and professional influences, and explores struggles, accomplishments, and contributions. A timeline highlights the most significant life events against an historical perspective. Bibliographies supplement the reference value of each volume.

PREFACE

Ulysses S. Grant emerged from the Civil War as a national hero and a man of famed stature throughout the civilized world. Today, he is remembered by many as the general who won the war for the Union, the 18th president of the United States, or the man whose face adorns the front of the $50 bill. Grant has been immortalized in literary works. He has been portrayed on stage and screen by numerous actors, and his name has been given to schools, parks, and streets throughout the land. All of my formative years were spent with a constant reminder of the regard with which Ulysses S. Grant is held. The little town where I was born and raised, Salisbury, Pennsylvania, was incorporated in 1862. The sentiment of the local citizens can readily be found in the names they gave to the three principal streets in the newly formed borough. One was called Union Avenue, to symbolize the cause they upheld. The second was named Ord Street, in honor of General Edward O. C. Ord, from nearby Cumberland, Maryland. The last street in the town, the main street, was named Grant Street, in tribute to the new national hero who had just captured Forts Henry and Donelson and had become known throughout the land as "Unconditional Surrender" Grant. The neighboring towns, on either side of Salisbury, had also decided to name their main street Grant Street.

But who was this military conqueror and political giant? Grant, the man, bore precious little resemblance to the dominant and decisive figure depicted in most of the biographical writings that concentrated on his life in the years immediately following the end of the war. He was an unlikely hero, and few, if any, of his contemporaries would have predicted greatness in his future. In fact, he was the poster child for the assurance American parents have given their children for almost 200 years that "anyone can grow up to be President." Ulysses Simpson Grant was not even his real name. It was a mistake, made in his adolescence, that was never corrected. Though he won everlasting fame on the battlefield, Grant never felt at home in the army. Later in life he would state, "The truth is I am more a farmer than a soldier. I take little or no interest in military affairs. I never went into the army without regret and never retired without pleasure." Grant's rise to fame in the military would have seemed ludicrous to most of his peers in the old army. He had been forced to retire, or face the humiliation of a public court martial, owing to an incident of public drunkenness that took place in 1852. From that point on, Grant was labeled by many of the officers he would later serve with in the Civil War. When his name would come up in conversation, it would usually be followed by a smug facial expression and the inevitable comment, "He drinks." Civilian life proved to be an extension of his military disappointment, and Grant moved from failure to failure until he was finally forced to accept a menial position in his father's leather tannery, a profession he loathed. The outbreak of hostilities in the Civil War found Grant and his family almost destitute, with very little promise for positive change in either his personal or professional fortunes. While many men hungered for glory and greatness as a result of the war, Grant saw the national calamity as merely a chance to make himself useful and to utilize the education he had received at the public's expense, at West Point.

Grant, the man, was a very plain and common individual. A story is told of a young newspaper boy who was selling biographies of Grant on a train the general happened to be riding on. Grant was on his way to Washington to meet with Lincoln and accept his commission as lieutenant general and his assignment as general-in-chief of the

army. When one of Grant's staff officers pointed out the general to
the newspaper boy, he was met with ridicule from the lad, who could
not believe that the unassuming, ordinary-looking man seated before
him was indeed the hero of Donelson, Henry, Shiloh, Vicksburg, and
Chattanooga. Another story concerning Grant's disdain for adornment
centers on the surrender ceremonies at Appomattox Courthouse. General Robert E. Lee appeared at the meeting dressed in his finest uniform
and looking every bit the military hero. Grant, in contrast, arrived in
a mud-spattered private's blouse, looking more like a soldier from the
ranks than the commanding general of all the Union armies. Many
biographers cite this as an example of Grant, the common man, versus
Lee, the aristocrat. A look at Grant's life, however, will show that this
was the manifestation of a character trait that was deeply embedded
in the general. Shortly after his graduation from West Point, Grant
had gone home to Bethel, Ohio, to visit his family. Proud of his accomplishment and feeling, no doubt, like the town's favorite son, he
anticipated a hero's welcome from the inhabitants. He was dressed in
the finest tailored officer's uniform he could afford and looked for all
the world like a great man. Much to his surprise, he was greeted by a
young boy who taunted and jeered at him because of his military finery.
Another local resident hastily threw together a homemade caricature
of Grant's uniform and paraded up and down the street making fun of
the mortified officer. Grant would say that "the joke was a high one in
the mind of many people, and was much enjoyed by them; but I did not
appreciate it so highly." From that day forward, Grant abstained from
any show of military grandeur and was generally to be found wearing
the uniform of a private, with his insignia of rank attached. A reticent
and introverted man, Grant was easily embarrassed and did not suffer
humiliation lightly. It was a character trait that would surface many
times in his life. In many ways, Grant's fame was a source of discomfort.
The general's personality was far more conducive to being a nondescript officer, serving within the army, not the commanding general of
that army, where he would be constantly the object of public censure
and condemnation.

What Grant may have lacked in confidence he made up for with
another strong character trait: determination. An individual who met
Grant for the first time, during the war, described this feature in graphic

tone when he said that the general looked like a man who had decided to ram his head through a brick wall and was just about to do it.
Determination and perseverance were the hallmarks of Grant's success. It was because of these that he was able to maintain a oneness
of purpose that resulted in a resolve to see the war through to its final
conclusion, to fight it out to the bitter end, despite the ever-increasing
cost in lives and treasure. This determination would never be more in
evidence than in the final days of his life. Following his presidency,
Grant found himself once more destitute and without the means to
support his family. Faulty financial management, combined with poor
investments, had decimated his financial holdings and left him all but
penniless. When a New York publisher offered a substantial advance
for his memoirs, Grant saw it as a final opportunity to make sure that
his family was provided for. But by this time, he was already suffering
from advanced stages of throat cancer, and it was quite probable that
he would not survive long enough to complete the arduous task of compiling his autobiography. The general who had battled upon so many
fields in the Civil War faced the toughest fight of his life as he struggled
to finish the manuscript before death's dark shadow cast its pall over
him. The general won his final battle, working through excruciating
pain and mental torment, and completed the autobiography just seven
days before his death. He would not live to see the book published, but
he had succeeded in providing a source of income for his family after
he was gone. His memoirs sold 300,000 copies in its first printing and
would eventually earn some $450,000 in royalties for his widow and
their children.

Personal Memoirs of U.S. Grant, volumes 1 and 2, published by
Charles L. Webster Publishing in 1885, has been relied on heavily in
the writing of this biography, as Grant's memoirs provide an insight into
the mind of the man that can be garnered in no other way. Additional
insight is provided through the biographical works penned by two of
his closest and most trusted staff officers. Military History of Ulysses S.
Grant, volumes 1 and 2, written by Adam Badeau and published by
D. Appleton and Company in 1868, and Campaigning with Grant, written by Horace Porter and published by the Century Company in 1897,
both provide glimpses of Grant from these observant subordinates who
were in daily contact with the general during the war. I have consulted

numerous Grant biographies in compiling this book. Possibly the best and most balanced of these is *Grant: A Biography*, written by William S. McFeely and published by W. W. Norton and Company in 1981. A more complete disclosure of sources used in writing this book is included in the bibliographical essay at the end of this work.

The purpose of this book is to provide the reader with a factual and balanced biography of this famed military and political leader who was involved in so many epic events in our nation's history. It is not the intention of the author to write a tribute or a eulogy or to gloss over character faults or human frailties to pay homage to Grant. Instead, it is my objective to give a fair and balanced biography that tells the complete story of his life, the victories and the failures, the triumphs and the tragedies, and shows how this common man of the people attained greatness, sometimes in spite of himself, through quiet determination and unshaken will.

I would like to thank Bob Redman for sharing his particular insight regarding Grant and his contemporaries and for his help in pointing me toward sources that discard the myth and legend and deal only with truth and facts. History is supposed to be the recording of what actually took place, not a transcription of events as we would like to remember them or as some would have us remember them.

TIMELINE: EVENTS IN THE LIFE OF ULYSSES S. GRANT

April 27, 1822	Born in Point Pleasant, Ohio.
May 1839	Enters the U.S. Military Academy at West Point.
1843	Graduates from West Point and receives a lieutenant's commission in the 4th U.S. Infantry.
September 30, 1843	Reports to Jefferson Barracks.
February 1844	Meets Julia Dent.
September 1845	Enters Texas with Zachary Taylor's army.
September 22, 1846	Fights in the Battle of Monterrey.
September 14, 1847	American army captures Mexico City and ends the Mexican-American War.
August 22, 1848	He and Julia Dent are married.
May 30, 1850	Frederick Dent Grant is born.
July 22, 1852	Ulysses S. Grant Jr. is born.
July 31, 1854	Resigns from the army and begins civilian life.
June 15, 1861	Assumes command of the 21st Illinois Regiment.
August 1862	Promoted to the rank of brigadier general.

February 1862	Captures Forts Henry and Donelson. Promoted to the rank of major general.
April 6–7, 1862	Fights the Battle of Shiloh.
April 25, 1862	Replaced by George H. Thomas as commander of the Army of the Tennessee.
July 10, 1862	Reinstated to commander of the army when General Henry Halleck is called to Washington.
September 19, 1862	The Battle of Iuka is fought by a portion of Grant's command.
October 4, 1862	The Battle of Corinth is fought by a portion of Grant's command.
December 20, 1862	Grant's supply base at Holly Springs, Mississippi, is destroyed by General Earl Van Dorn.
December 28, 1862	Sherman's assault at Chickasaw Bayou is repulsed.
January 9, 1863	A portion of Grant's command, under General John McClernand, captures Arkansas Post.
January 17, 1863	Grant arrives at the front to take command of the army and formally undertake the campaign against Vicksburg.
March 29, 1863	Grant orders the construction of a road on the Louisiana side of the Mississippi to march his army below Vicksburg.
April 16, 1863	Flag Officer David Porter's gunboats successfully run past the Confederate batteries at Vicksburg.
April 30, 1863	Grant successfully transfers a portion of his army across the Mississippi River to Bruinsburg, Mississippi.
May 1, 1863	Grant is victorious in the Battle of Port Gibson.
May 12, 1863	Grant's army defeats a portion of General Joseph Johnston's army at the Battle of Raymond.
May 14, 1863	Grant's army captures the city of Jackson, Mississippi.

May 16, 1863   Grant defeats General John Pemberton's army at the Battle of Champion's Hill.

May 17, 1863   Grant again emerges victorious against Pemberton at the Battle of the Big Black River.

May 19, 1863   Grant orders a general assault against the city of Vicksburg. It is repulsed.

May 22, 1863   Grant makes a second large-scale attack against Vicksburg. It is unsuccessful, prompting him to lay siege to the city.

July 4, 1863   General Pemberton surrenders his army, and the city of Vicksburg, to Grant.

October 23, 1863   Grant arrives in Chattanooga to take command of Union forces.

November 25, 1863   Confederate forces at Chattanooga are defeated in the battles of Lookout Mountain and Missionary Ridge.

March 3, 1864   Grant is called east to be promoted to the rank of lieutenant general.

May 5, 1864   Grant confronts Robert E. Lee's Army of Northern Virginia in the Wilderness.

May 11–18, 1864   The Army of the Potomac battles with the Confederates at Spotsylvania Court House.

June 3, 1864   Grant orders a frontal assault on the Confederate defenses at Cold Harbor. The attack is repulsed with heavy losses.

June 1864   Union and Confederate forces come together on the outskirts of Richmond and Petersburg. Grant is unable to break through the Southern defenses and lays siege to Lee's army. The armies would be locked in a death struggle that would last for more than nine months.

April 9, 1865   Grant meets with Robert E. Lee at Appomattox Court House to give terms of surrender for the Army of Northern Virginia.

1866   Congress revives the rank of full general in the army and bestows the honor on Grant.

May 20, 1868	Grant receives the nomination of the Republican Party as its candidate for president.
November 1868	Grant wins the fall election to become the 18th president of the United States.
November 1872	Grant wins reelection to his second term as president.
May 1877	Grant embarks on his world tour. He would not return to America for over two years.
May 1884	Grant is left penniless in the Marine National Bank scandal. An offer from Mark Twain to publish his memoirs provides a source of income and a way to provide for his family.
July 23, 1885	Grant dies at his home at Mount McGregor, New York, about a week after he finishes his memoirs.

Chapter 1

ANCESTORS, LINEAGE, AND EARLY YEARS

The Grant family had resided in America for almost 200 years by the time Ulysses S. Grant was born. Matthew Grant had come across the ocean from England in 1630 to settle in Dorchester, Massachusetts. In 1635, he moved to what is now Windsor, Connecticut, where he became surveyor for the colony for some four decades. Descendants of Matthew Grant have lived in the Windsor area for centuries. Ulysses's great-grandfather Noah Grant was a representative New Englander of his era, and when the French and Indian War erupted, he and his younger brother, Soloman, volunteered to fight for the British. Both were killed in 1756. Ulysses's grandfather, also named Noah, was only eight years old when his father was killed and the responsibilities of manhood were thrust upon him. In his autobiography, Ulysses states that his grandfather was a hero of the American Revolution and had fought in numerous engagements in that struggle, from Bunker Hill to Yorktown. According to his grandson, he had risen to the rank of captain in the Continental Army and had distinguished himself on many hard-fought fields of battle. It is unclear exactly where Grant got his information concerning his grandfather. Possibly it came from the old gentleman himself. What is certain is that there are no records to substantiate that he ever served a single day in the army. Some historians have offered the suggestion that, over the years, confusion took place between this Noah Grant and his father, who bore the same name and was indeed a captain in the army.

It is certain, however, that shortly after the conclusion of the Revolutionary War, Noah Grant moved from New England to Westmoreland County, Pennsylvania, near the present-day city of Greensburg. Life in Connecticut had become troublesome for Noah. His wife, Anne Richardson, had died, leaving him a widower with two boys. Land speculation had caused him to amass debts that would eventually result in his being thrown in debtor's prison and would necessitate that he sell his holdings in Connecticut to settle affairs with his creditors. Noah's eldest son was fully grown and remained in Connecticut. His youngest, Peter, accompanied him to Westmoreland County.

In 1792, Noah married Rachael Kelly, Ulysses's grandmother. Noah and Rachael would have five children together. Jesse Root Grant, their second child and Ulysses S. Grant's father, was born on January 23, 1794. In 1799, Noah moved his family to East Liverpool, Ohio, in the eastern portion of the state. In 1804, the Grants moved again, this time to Deerfield, Ohio, where Noah earned a living by making shoes. Rachael Grant died in Deerfield in 1805. The death of Rachael Grant caused a severe hardship on the family. Noah had been scratching out a living ever since his financial troubles back in Connecticut, and Rachael's passing found the Grants so poor that Noah was unable to provide for his family. His younger children were sent to live with more prosperous relatives, while the older ones, including Jesse, now 11 years old, were apprenticed out to various families to learn a trade. Jesse was apprenticed to George Tod of Youngstown, Ohio, a judge at the local courthouse and the father of David Tod, who would serve as governor of the state during the Civil War. Evidently, Jesse's time with the Tods was a pleasant experience. In his autobiography, Ulysses S. Grant states that his father "looked upon Judge Tod and his wife, with all the reverence he could have felt if they had been his parents instead of benefactors." Jesse remained with the Tods for only a few years before relocating to Maysville, Kentucky. His half brother Peter Grant had established a tannery in Maysville and took Jesse under his wing, teaching him all he needed to know about the trade of tanning leather. Once his training was complete, Jesse moved back to Deerfield to establish himself. He initially accepted work and lodging with the family of Owen Brown, a tanner in Deerfield. Owen was the father of John Brown, of Harpers Ferry fame, and Jesse had the opportunity to get to know the boy quite well while they were living under the same roof. Jesse thought that John Brown was "a man of great purity of character, of high moral and physical courage, but a fanatic and extremist in whatever he advocated."

After spending enough time working for the Browns to save a little money, Jesse moved to Ravenna, Ohio, where he established a tannery of his own. A few years later, he moved the business to Point Pleasant, Ohio, where his efforts were crowned with success. The tannery became so profitable that Jesse was able to buy large tracts of land in the Point Pleasant area and establish himself as a respectable and prosperous member of the community. Ulysses would describe his father's stature by saying that he was, "from my earliest recollection, in comfortable circumstances, considering the times, his place of residence, and the community in which he lived." By eastern standards, Jesse Grant would probably have been considered little more than a laborer, but in the growing town of Deerfield, he was looked upon as a man of substance and a pillar of the community.

In June 1821, the 27-year-old Jesse Grant wed Hannah Simpson. The Simpsons were a respected family in the Point Pleasant area. Hannah's parents, John and Rebecca, had moved to Ohio from Berks County, Pennsylvania. They owned 600 acres of land in the Ohio Valley and were considered to be affluent and intellectual. Hannah herself remains something of a mystery to Grant biographers. She seems to have been a reserved and introverted woman, quite the opposite of her outgoing and gregarious husband. She was never known to have granted an interview to a member of the press and seemed to be constantly shielded from the public by the Grant family. This has led some historians to speculate that Hannah might possibly have been simple-minded or have suffered from some sort of mental illness. It is known that Hannah Grant was an extremely pious Methodist who trusted all events in her life to the will of God. She has been described as an indifferent and introverted woman, but those tendencies could also be ascribed to a serene faith that kept her from experiencing the emotional highs and lows felt by those who have not consigned their lives to a higher power. While Ulysses S. Grant wrote at great length about his father in his memoirs, he made no mention of his mother. There were no stories of tenderness, no recollections of motherly care or comfort as are usually to be found in autobiographies. In fact, of the more than 1,200 pages that he wrote for his autobiography, only eight are dedicated to the story of his childhood. The omission of any stories about his mother is compounded by the fact that he does not mention the name of one childhood friend or companion. Apart from his siblings, Grant seems to have led a lonely and isolated life.

On April 27, 1822, Jesse and Hannah Grant welcomed the birth of their first child. The naming of the child became a matter of negotiation and compromise for the family, and it would be fully six weeks before the task was accomplished. Hannah was fond of the name Ulysses. Her mother had read her a translation of the epic *Telemachus* when she was a girl, and Ulysses was her favorite character in the book. Jesse Grant was willing to concede that Ulysses be part of the child's name, but he felt it unsuited for a first name. Hiram seemed to him to be a manlier-sounding name. In the end, the infant was named Hiram Ulysses Grant, but Hannah adopted Ulysses as the name by which he was commonly called around the house.

Eighteen months after Ulysses's birth, the family relocated to Georgetown, Ohio, where Jesse Grant built a new tannery and a small but sturdy brick house for the family. Five more children were born to the Grants at Georgetown: Samuel Simpson in 1825, Clara Rachael in 1828, Virginia Paine in 1832, Orvil Lynch in 1835, and Mary Frances in 1839. Jesse Grant's business flourished in Georgetown. His financial success allowed him to provide for his ever-expanding family by building a wing on his house that was larger than the original structure had been. Jesse also became involved in local organizations and politics. In 1830, he was made master of the Masonic lodge in Georgetown. In 1837, he was elected mayor of the town. A lifelong Jacksonian Democrat, he had split with the party to become a Whig before his election.

Jesse was aggressive, outspoken, and a force to be reckoned with in local affairs. Ulysses did not favor his father in these personality or character traits. He more closely mirrored the qualities of his mother, being a reticent and introverted young boy. Ulysses surely disappointed his father through his hatred of the tanning business. The tannery was just across the street from Ulysses's bedroom, and he was haunted by the cries of the animals that were killed for their hides. The stench from the tannery permeated every room in the house, and Ulysses never seemed to get used to it. He later wrote, "I detested the trade, preferring almost any other labor." Jesse did not force his son to follow in his footsteps. Instead, the boy was permitted to contribute to the family in other ways. Jesse owned a great deal of land around Georgetown, including some 50 acres of wooded property just outside of town. "When I was seven or eight years old," Grant wrote, "I began hauling all the wood used in the house and shops. I could not load it on the wagons, of course, at that time, but I could drive, and the choppers would load, and someone at the house unload." By the time he was 11, Grant took on the responsibility for plowing and tending the cultivated fields of the family. The common denominator in both occupations was the use of horses. Ulysses exhibited a talent for working with horses at a very early age. He showed an affection for animals that probably was exaggerated by the gruesome reality of his father's tannery business. Jesse recognized his son's knack with horses, and he allowed the boy a great deal of latitude in training and working the animals. Ulysses once made a trade for a new horse that was skittish and unused to working in harness. He had hitched the animal up to his wagon and started for home, and all was going well until they came across a dog that startled the animal and caused it to buck and kick violently. Grant was able to calm the animal, and after a short rest, he once again started out for home. But the horse had other ideas. He bolted uncontrollably and almost plunged wagon and driver over a steep embankment, with Ulysses able to stop him only "on the very brink of the precipice." Every time Grant would try to start out again, the horse would begin to kick and buck violently. The boy was apparently stranded with an animal that would not obey his commands, but then Ulysses got an idea. He took out his bandana and "blindfolded my horse." The animal was transformed at once from a raging terrified beast into a docile and obedient servant.

Another story is told about a circus that visited Georgetown when Grant was a boy. The circus had a trick pony that the owner claimed could not be ridden. The pony's mane had been cut and its back was greased, and it had been trained to throw anyone who attempted to ride it. A prize of five dollars was proclaimed for anyone who was able to remain seated on the animal. One by one, the young men of Georgetown lined up to test their mettle against the pony, all with the same result. Finally, young Ulysses took his turn. He climbed aboard the animal's back and, clasping his arms around its neck, hung on like a bulldog as the owner cracked his whip at the pony's hooves and commanded it through its progressive routine of tricks. The young rider would not be unhorsed, and in the end, he was rewarded for his efforts with the five-dollar prize. Grant's love of horses, and his aptitude at working with them, would continue throughout his life and would provide him with pleasure and a sense of accomplishment.

Although Grant conscientiously and industrially completed his labors, he was not at all fond of them. Indeed, he once stated that laziness was "my besetting sin through life." "I did not like to work," he later wrote, "but did as much of it, while young, as grown men can be hired to do in these days." Like it or not, the menial labors he performed were numerous but must have been preferable to working in his father's tanning business.

Ulysses seems to have been something of an introvert and a loner as he was growing up. He felt more at ease with horses than he did with people. Quiet and self-contained, he was neither a leader nor a follower when it came to interacting with children his own age. He was short and thin for his age. In the rustic setting of the Ohio Valley, the boys were as tough and unrefined as their surroundings. Profanity was seen as a mark of distinction among the boys in Georgetown, and respect was given to the most prolific cussers in the town. Grant never took up the practice, and there is no record of him ever using a swear word in his life. In many ways, he was an easy target for childhood taunting by his peers. Ulysses would receive his first of many nicknames from the boys in Georgetown, and though it was probably hurtful, it was mercifully short-lived. The boys around town took to calling him "Useless" instead of Ulysses. Later in life, Ulysses would comment on the teasing he endured while a young boy, and one can easily see that it left a lasting mark upon him. "Boys enjoy the misery of their companions, at least village boys in that day did, and in later life I have found that all adults are not free from the peculiarity."

Jesse Grant saw to it that young Ulysses received a proper educa-tion by sending the boy to a number of tuition schools in the area. Free, public education had not yet emerged in the Ohio Valley, and the schools that existed were funded through subscription by the families whose children attended them. Most of Grant's school years were spent in Georgetown, attending the school run by John D. White of North Carolina. During the 1836–1837 school year, he stayed with relatives in Maysville and attended the Richardson and Rand Academy. The 1838–1839 school year found him taking classes in a school in Ripley, Ohio. Although Ulysses stated that he had never been punished at home, such was not the case at school. "The rod was freely used there, and I was not exempt from its influence. I can see John D. White—the school teacher—now, with his long beech switch always in hand." By eastern standards, Grant's education would have been considered mod-est, but it was advanced for a region that had recently been the fron-tier and provided him with the fundamentals in reading, writing, and arithmetic that would stand him in good stead in later life.

Chapter 2

THE SCHOOL OF
THE SOLDIER

During the school year of 1838–1839, while Ulysses was attending classes in Ripley, Jesse Grant took it upon himself to secure his son's future by obtaining an appointment to the U.S. Military Academy, at West Point, for him. Jesse was self-taught, and he seemed determined to provide his son with the education he was not able to acquire. It is interesting, however, that Ulysses was the only one of his children that he actively pushed into the academic world. Ulysses's sisters all stayed home, and his brothers entered the family business and learned the tanning trade. Possibly Jesse pushed young Ulysses to get his education because he knew that he would never join the rest of the family in the tannery and he worried about how the boy would earn a living when he became a man. It is certain that his actions were not motivated by any admiration for the military on his part because Jesse seemed to favor the accomplishments of his sons who had gone into the tannery over those of his soldier son for many years. What is certain is that Jesse contacted Senator Charles Morris seeking an appointment for his son. To his great disappointment, Morris, a fellow Whig, failed to provide the desired appointment. This caused Jesse to turn to Congressman Thomas Hamer, a political rival and member of the Democratic Party.

Hamer informed Jesse that there was indeed an opening at the academy as a result of the dismissal of Bartlett Bailey, a young man who had also hailed from Georgetown. Hamer agreed to give the appointment to Ulysses, and all was settled, as least so far as Jesse was concerned.

Away at school in Ripley, Ulysses had no idea of the plans his father was making for his future. He first learned of his appointment when he came home from school to celebrate Christmas vacation. During that holiday break, Jesse received a letter from Hamer confirming that all of the arrangements had been finalized and Ulysses had been given the appointment. Jesse read the letter and informed his son, "Ulysses, I believe you are going to receive the appointment." His son had no idea what appointment he was referring to, and when he asked his father to elaborate, Jesse said, "To West Point, I have applied for it." Ulysses was stunned by the revelation. "But I won't go," he declared. Jesse was quick to inform him that he would do as he was told, and Ulysses remembered, "He said he thought I would, and I thought so too, if he did." Grant's reluctance to accept the appointment did not stem from an aversion to the military. Instead, he felt himself ill-prepared and unworthy to attend such a prestigious institution. "I had a very exalted idea of the acquirements necessary to get through. I did not believe I possessed them, and could not bear the idea of failing."

While the prospects of academic failure hung over him like a cloud, Grant looked forward to going to West Point. "I had always a great desire to travel," he said, but it was the trip he anticipated, not his enrollment at the academy. Grant knew that he would get to see the sites in Philadelphia and New York City on his way to West Point, and he had always wanted to visit those places. So far as the academy was concerned, once his tour of the two great metropolises of the East was concluded, "I would have been glad to have a steamboat or railroad collision, or any other accident happen, by which I might have received a temporary injury sufficient to make me ineligible, for a time, to enter the Academy." No such intervention was to take place, however. In May 1839, Grant began his journey to West Point. He made extended stops in Philadelphia and New York, bringing a reprimand from his father, who felt he was "dallying" in arriving at his final destination. Finally, he reported at West Point on May 30 or 31 and began the process of examinations to determine if he was qualified for admittance. Two weeks later, much to his surprise, Grant was informed that he had passed the battery of tests and was to become a cadet.

The aspect of learning to become a soldier was not the only change that was taking place in Grant's life. Upon reporting to the academy, he underwent a change that would follow him for the rest of his days. When he reported to the admissions office, he did so as Hiram Ulysses Grant. The officer in charge soon informed him that there was no appointment on the rolls for any such person. He did, however, have an appointment for a Ulysses Simpson Grant. Congressman Hamer had known the boy by his mother's pet name, Ulysses, not as Hiram. He had accordingly submitted that as Grant's first name. Not knowing the boy's middle name, nor making the effort to learn it, he had written in Simpson, his mother's maiden name. The admissions officer was a by-the-book administrator, and he refused to make any changes to his roll. He had an appointment for a Ulysses Simpson Grant, not Hiram Ulysses Grant. If the young man wished to attend the academy, it would have to be under the name that was listed on the admission rolls. From that day forward, Ulysses Simpson Grant was the name by which he was known, and Hiram would become a forgotten bit of trivia for family members and historians. The alteration did not entirely meet with Grant's disapproval. On the way to West Point, he had begun making changes of his own. Upon checking in to a hotel along the way, he had already decided to go by his middle name and had signed in as U. H. Grant. He would continue to sign his name as Ulysses H. Grant for some time following the mix-up at the West Point admissions office but would eventually succumb to adopting Simpson in place of Hiram.

Grant was pleasantly surprised that he had passed his admission exams, but he held no illusions regarding his aptitude for military life. The prospect of failing, and being forced to return home in disgrace, still haunted the young cadet. When a bill was introduced in Congress, in December 1839, proposing the abolishment of West Point, Grant saw it as a way to get out of the academy without being dishonored and privately hoped the bill would be approved.

Several of the classmates Grant had been thrown together with would go on to achieve fame and distinction in the Civil War. Among the most notable members of the class that would graduate in 1843 were Samuel French, Rufus Ingalls, Roswell Ripley, and William B. Franklin. During his time at the academy, Grant would also make the acquaintance of other notable cadets, such as Winfield Scott Hancock, George B. McClellan, George E. Pickett, James P. Longstreet, Don Carlos Buell, Earl Van Dorn, William T. Sherman, and William S. Rosecrans. In fact, during his four-year stay at West Point, Grant would come in contact with more than 100 cadets who would later serve as generals in the Civil War. But glory and military distinction were little more than daydreams for these young men quartered along the banks of the Hudson River.

Grant's name had forever been changed by the admissions officer at the academy. He would also receive the nickname that would follow him for the rest of his life from one of his fellow cadets at West Point. William T. Sherman was supposedly perusing the list of new cadets when he came upon the name of U.S. Grant. The other cadets in the room speculated on what the U.S. stood for, and some were of the opinion that Grant's name must be United States. Sherman offered a differing opinion. He thought that the initials must stand for Uncle Sam. Thus, before Grant ever arrived at the academy, he had already received the nickname by which he would be known to his comrades in the military for as long as they all lived: Sam.

Grant seemed somewhat out of place at West Point. To begin with, he did not fit in with the spit-and-polish cadets who aspired to military glory and who modeled themselves after the great tacticians and leaders of the past. In his appearance, mannerisms, and speech, Grant was viewed as a country bumpkin, and his peers thought that he would amount to little as an officer. His unmilitary bearing dictated that he be assigned to the awkward squad, where he received remedial training to bring him up to par with the rest of the cadets. After a period of time, he was able to master sufficient military discipline to be graduated from this inglorious unit, but he never managed to attain a degree of proficiency that could be considered soldierly. The fact is Grant's mental abilities were not prone to thinking in precise or scientific terms. He was not an abstract thinker, and the conceptual realm of the military leader was beyond him. His mental process was of a more practical bent, a hands-on problem solver. He did not possess the vision of an architect to be able to see a building in his mind's eye, but he had the practical knowledge necessary to take a set of blueprints and construct a building from them.

In his studies and in his deportment, Grant showed an indifference that would seem to be a self-fulfilling prophesy to his fears of failure at the academy. Dr. Henry Coppee observed him during this time and said that he "exhibited but little enthusiasm for anything." He was described by a fellow cadet as being "not particularly tidy about his dress, and he even had a certain slouchy air about him that many of the class thought unsolder, but he never did anything positively offensive, and as he was always quiet and attended to his own affairs, we liked him well enough."

Grant's appearance and deportment would be a constant source of embarrassment to him during his time at West Point, though there is no evidence that he ever took steps to correct them. By the time of his graduation, his conduct ranking was only 156 out of a total number of 223 cadets at the academy. The vast majority of the demerits he received came as the result of slovenly dress. Improper uniform, unbuttoned garments, and stains on his clothes were continual complaints against him. He also amassed a large number of demerits for tardiness. A heavy sleeper, he was often to be found late for roll call.

In regard to his studies, Grant showed the same lack of attention that he did for his dress. The course work bored him, and he stated that he "rarely ever read over a lesson the second time during my entire cadetship." Instead of pouring over studies of French or mathematics or engrossing himself in military tactics or strategy, Grant spent most of his time reading popular novels of the day, obtained from the West Point library. James Fenimore Cooper and Washington Irving were among his favorite writers. Both men wrote about the Eastern Seaboard when it was still a frontier, and it is possible that reading their work provided Ulysses with an escape from the academy, a sort of vacation in his mind, back to his rustic and unbridled home in the Ohio Valley. No interest, however, was ever shown for works devoted to the vocation he was pursuing, as Grant never read a single book on military tactics or history in his entire lifetime.

Equestrian pursuits were naturally a strong point for Grant, and he ranked high in his class in horsemanship. His prowess on horseback was one of the few distinctions he earned at the academy and was his only claim to fame among his fellow cadets. This must have suited him just fine, however, as he aspired to receive a posting to the dragoons upon graduation, where he could use his abilities to their fullest.

The first two years at West Point passed by quickly, though Grant felt that they seemed "five times as long as an Ohio year," and after the June examinations, Ulysses received an extended furlough to go home. But his home had changed. Jesse had sold his business and house in Georgetown and had moved to Bethel, Ohio, 12 miles away, where he took up the occupation of farming. Even though the surroundings were foreign to him, Ulysses reveled in the chance to escape from the drudgery of West Point and remembered this time with his family for enjoyment "beyond any other period in my life." For a short time, he was free from the drums and bugles, free from the drill and inspections. His father had given him a new horse, and Ulysses spent much of his time exploring the countryside and enjoying his absolute freedom. The furlough passed much too quickly, and Grant complained that the 10 weeks seemed shorter than one at West Point. It must have been with a heavy heart that he reported back to the academy on August 28 to begin his third year of instruction.

It was undoubtedly with apprehension that Grant learned upon his return to West Point that he had been made a sergeant in the corps of cadets. The appointment was a source of ridicule from his classmates, who vowed that he had been made a sergeant because he could not keep in step during drill. As a sergeant, he would not be in the ranks and therefore could not throw his comrades out of step with his irregular cadence. Grant must have undertaken the assignment with great misgivings. He neither desired nor sought positions of command or leadership, and the responsibility surely caused him no small amount of discomfort. His superiors at West Point evidently shared in his discomfort, for at the conclusion of his third year, Grant was dropped from the roll of sergeants and returned to the ranks of the privates. His brief time in command had shown no promise of leadership potential.

During his senior year at the academy, Ulysses had another diversion to occupy his idle hours and intrigue his mind. Robert Weir was a professor on the faculty, charged with teaching the cadets to draw and paint. It was felt that officers should be given the rudimentary skills of drawing so that they could sketch features of terrain or objects of military interest, such as bridges or fortifications. Grant was very fond of this course and devoted himself to mastering it, as he did with no other field of study during his time at West Point. Weir was an excellent teacher who would go on to instruct the famed American artist James Whistler, and he touched Grant as no other instructor at the academy was able to do. Grant displayed a proficiency for drawing equal to his passion for it and spent a great deal of time in the studio painting. He attempted a wide array of subject matter, eventually mastering the techniques necessary to paint landscapes, animals, and people.

Grant's final year at West Point passed as uneventfully as the previous three had been. He would hold his own in his studies, and in the end, he would find himself ranked in the middle of his class, graduating 21st out of a class of 39. Although he had managed to make himself acceptable to his classmates, Grant had created no real lasting friendships during his time at West Point. The introverted characteristics that had defined his youth continued as he grew into manhood. His name would not be among the first to come to mind when classmates recalled their days along the Hudson, as he had passed the four years in relative obscurity, little noticed by his peers. But Grant had noticed his peers. Even if he did not have the social skills needed to cultivate friendships or favorably position himself among the hierarchy of hopeful young officers, he possessed the perception to judge and evaluate the character and merits of many of the men who would later become leaders in the Civil War. His quiet observations would serve him well when leadership was finally thrust upon him.

Each graduating cadet was required to submit a listing, in order of preference, for his assignment in the regular army. Naturally, Grant placed the 1st U.S. Dragoons at the top of his list. But the 1st Dragoons was the only regiment of cavalry in the U.S. Army at that time, and there were no vacancies to be filled in its corps of officers. The 4th U.S. Infantry was Grant's second choice, and it was to this unit that he would ultimately be assigned.

Grant must have been surprised to actually be among those receiving a degree from the academy. He had been so sure that his failure at West Point was preordained and had shown precious little concern for learning his studies. His time at the academy had not changed his mind

Ulysses S. Grant appears here following his graduation from West Point, as a brevet second lieutenant in the 4th U.S. Infantry. (U.S. Army Military History Institute)

regarding a career in the military either. Once his mandatory tour of duty was complete, Grant planned to resign his commission and seek employment as a professor at some credible college. Still, West Point had not failed to impress Ulysses, and he gained a lifelong, if grudging, respect for the principles the institution stood for. "I think West Point is the finest school in the world," he would later state. "I do not mean the highest grade, but the most thorough in its discipline. A boy to go through four years in West Point must have the essential elements of a strong, manly character. Lacking any of these he must fail. I hear army men say their happiest days were at West Point. I never had that experience. The most trying days of my life were those I spent there, and I never recall them with pleasure."

Chapter 3

THE WAR WITH MEXICO

Grant's assignment to the 4th U.S. Infantry meant that he would be stationed at Jefferson Barracks, Missouri, just a short distance south of St. Louis. Along the way to the post, the new lieutenant was granted time for a short visit with his family in Bethel. Regardless of his ambivalence toward his time at West Point, Grant was genuinely proud of the fact that he had managed to complete the course of studies, and he could hardly wait to impress his family and neighbors with his accomplishment. He had placed an order for a new uniform with a tailor, but the completion of the work was delayed until it was determined if the uniform should be for the cavalry or the infantry. With his posting confirmed, the tailor finished the garment with the appropriate trappings for a new lieutenant foot officer. This uniform was a great deal larger than the one he had been issued when he first reported at the academy. Grant had experienced more than intellectual growth at West Point. He had been a slight five feet, one inch when he reported as a plebe of cadets. Four years later, he had shot up to a height of five feet, eight inches.

On his way to Bethel, Grant passed through Cincinnati, where he came across a young boy standing along the main street. Grant straightened himself in his saddle and tried to evince all of the military splendor he could muster, expecting to astound the lad with his martial bearing. Much to his chagrin, the boy began to hurl insulting barbs at him: "Soldier! Will you work? No, sir-ee; I'll sell my shirt first!" When he arrived in Bethel, Grant's reception was more in line with what he had anticipated. For most of the citizens of the town, this was the first army officer they had ever seen, and many of them did not know the difference between a lieutenant and a general. Grant enjoyed something of a celebrity status among the townspeople, and he was even asked to put the local militia company through its paces in a public drill. When the appointed day for the drill arrived, people from all over the region came to witness it. Observers noted how much smaller Grant was compared to the other officers in the militia. They also remembered that the young lieutenant seemed pale and nervous as he issued commands to the troops.

Grant did not find universal admiration among the citizens of Bethel, however. The stable man at the local tavern saw to it that Grant did not get carried away with adulation by directing a bit of satire in his direction. The man donned a pair of light-blue pants, "just the color of my uniform trousers—with a strip of white cotton sheeting sewed down the outside seams in imitation of mine." The man paraded himself up and down the streets of the town, mocking the embarrassed young lieutenant and issuing orders to make-believe soldiers. Grant wrote, "The joke was a huge one in the mind of many of the people, and was much enjoyed by them, but I did not appreciate it so highly." This incident, combined with the one involving the young boy in Cincinnati, served to sour Grant on any future shows of military finery. From then on, he would adorn himself in the plainest military dress available, usually a private's uniform with his insignia of rank attached.

When Grant concluded his short visit in Bethel, he made his way to Missouri and Jefferson Barracks, and on September 30, 1843, he reported for duty. In 1826, a military post was established near the Mississippi River, 10 miles south of St. Louis. In 1827, it was named Jefferson Barracks in honor of Thomas Jefferson, who had died the previous year. It was originally designated as an infantry school of practice, but in 1832, the U.S. Dragoons also made it their base of operations. That same year witnessed the first time that troops from Jefferson Barracks saw active duty, when they took part in the Black Hawk War. The post was both gracious and spacious. Numerous buildings surrounded a well-manicured parade ground, with other structures fanning out across the more than 1,700 acres that had been purchased for the post. By the time Grant arrived at Jefferson Barracks, it had grown to become the largest military post in the United States.

Life was uneventful and monotonous for the officers and men at Jefferson Barracks. Apart from the daily drilling of the men, there was little to occupy the off-duty hours of the men in the ranks or the officers who commanded them. Grant was to be rescued from the dull drudgery by a classmate from West Point, whose family lived in St. Louis. Frederick T. Dent had been in Grant's graduating class in 1843. The two cadets had shared little in common in terms of background, upbringing, or social views, but they did have one very strong bond. Neither Grant nor Dent had envisioned a career in the military, and both were perfectly content just to have graduated from the academy. As luck would have it, Dent and Grant were both assigned to the 4th Infantry, and both were posted to Jefferson Barracks. Dent saw to it that his family sent an invitation to Grant to come and visit them and spend some pleasant time away from the dull and tedious post.

The Dents were nothing like Grant's own family or any of the neighbors he had known in Ohio. They were a Southern family, with Southern ideals and traditions. They lived at White Haven, and though the name would lead one to believe it was a spacious estate, it was little more than a family farm. The occupants were what made this farm different than any Grant had ever seen before. Dent's father, also named Frederick T. Dent, was universally referred to as Colonel, though no one really knew if he had ever served in the military or of the title was simply a Southern show of respect. Colonel Dent ran his estate with all of the grace and charm that is normally associated with Southern gentry. Though his holdings and possessions were probably no more than Jesse Grant owned, Dent conducted himself like a Southern gentleman. The colonel and his entire family welcomed Grant to their home with a feeling of hospitality that the young lieutenant had never experienced before. They were courteous, caring, and, above all, comfortable—in sharp contrast to the home Grant had known. Ulysses found the Dents to be charming, and he looked forward to his visits with the family with great anticipation.

The Southern lifestyle of the Dents also accounted for the main difference between this family and any Grant had known before. The Dents owned slaves, and this was the first time that Ulysses had ever been in close contact with slaveholders. His own family was strongly opposed to slavery, and he had been raised to look upon the institution as a moral sin and a crime against God and nature. One might naturally conclude that Grant faced an inner struggle caused by a collision of moral values when his abolitionist upbringing came face to face with a slaveholding family. Quite the opposite seems to be true, however. Grant never recorded any evidence that would lead one to believe such an inner conflict ever existed. Instead, he records in his memoirs that his visits to the family were frequent and highly enjoyable. It is obvious that the Dents' status as slaveholders was never an issue to Grant. After a few months of bonding with the family, Grant got to meet the final member of the Dent household in February 1844. Colonel Dent's daughter, Julia, had been attending school at Professor Moreau's Academy, where she was learning English literature, French, music, and ballroom etiquette. Born on January 26, 1826, she had just turned 18 years of age when Ulysses first made her acquaintance.

Julia could hardly have been called a beauty. Although she was not plump or overweight, her figure has been described as being stumpy, having too much neck and not enough chin. She suffered from a malady known as strabismus, a condition where both eyes do not work in unison. In Julia's case, her right eye was prone to moving up and down involuntarily. But she had a pleasant way of speaking, was affable in her interactions with others, and tried to portray an air of femininity despite an unfeminine appearance. Julia was very athletic and enjoyed riding, hunting, and fishing with her brothers. She also enjoyed reading novels, including many of the same books that Grant had read at West Point. Their taste in literature, as well as the love of riding, was probably the first connection between the two, as they formed an immediate bond. The pair also shared personality traits of fearing failure and aspiring to accomplishments and positions of status that would ensure approval from others. Ulysses and Julia became inseparable, and a majority of Grant's time spent visiting the Dents was in her company.

Grant was not a romantic in any sense of the word. He had thus far in his life managed to steer clear of involvement with women because of either indifference or fear of rejection. It is known that he never attended any of the dances held at West Point, at which young ladies were invited to mingle with the cadets. He had never had a serious relationship with a girl, and it is doubtful if he had ever so much as been on anything that could be considered a date before meeting Julia. In her, he had found a companion and a kindred spirit, but Grant himself was not yet aware that he had found more.

As for Julia, almost from the start, she had decided that the young lieutenant was the man for her, and she set out to win his heart. As was the custom of the time, she named her bedpost after her intended beau and recorded in her memoirs that she had dreamed of "Mr. Grant." In the fall of 1844, Ulysses was granted a short leave to go home to visit his family in Ohio. The thought of being separated from Julia caused him to take an action that he had not anticipated. Sitting on the veranda at White Haven, he offered her his West Point class ring, but she flirtatiously refused to accept it, telling Ulysses that she was too young and that her mother would not approve. Later that night, Julia had a change of heart and rode to Jefferson Barracks, but Grant had already left for Bethel.

While Grant was back in Ohio, the U.S. military took steps to intervene in the border dispute that was taking place between the Republic of Texas and Mexico. Public opinion had been split over the Texas issue ever since the republic had won its independence. Those who were opposed wanted to avoid an armed conflict with Mexico, but they also wished to prevent the large landmass of Texas from being brought into the Union as a slave state, according to the provisions of the Missouri Compromise. Many Northerners speculated that Texas would be broken up into several states, altering the balance of power in Congress for generations to come in favor of the South. Most Southerners favored admitting Texas into the Union. Cotton was king, and the addition of this vast new territory would create untold opportunities to expand the plantation system into the Southwest. They were not afraid of a war with Mexico. In fact, they welcomed such a conflict. If Mexico was to be defeated, there could be additional land that might be ceded to the United States. Mexico itself might become part of the United States. Supporters claimed that eminent domain was the providence of the nation, that America's destiny was to control all the land from the Atlantic Ocean to the Pacific.

In the presidential election of 1844, James K. Polk was declared the winner. Polk was a Southern Democrat and an advocate of annexing Texas into the Union. His election set in motion a series of events that led to a joint resolution of Congress on February 26, 1845, that of-fered Texas the status of statehood in the Union. This action brought about a military response from the Mexican government, which had declined to recognize the independence Texas had been granted in the peace treaty signed by General Santa Anna following his defeat at the Battle of San Jacinto. So far as Mexico was concerned, Texas was still one of its possessions. Any action on the part of the Mexicans to forc-ibly take control of Texas would bring on a confrontation with the United States, however. Instead, the Mexican government determined to dispute the boundaries of the Texas Republic, claiming that the re-gion between the Rio Grande and the Nueces River still belonged to Mexico. The offer of annexation from Washington meant that it was now or never if the Mexican government wanted to press their territo-rial claims before Texas accepted the offer for statehood. The Mexican army was massed along the Texas border, and the armed forces of the United States were mobilized to respond to the threat.

Back at Jefferson Barracks, the 4th Infantry received orders to report immediately to western Louisiana, close to the Texas border. Grant was still on leave when his regiment departed, though he had left Ohio and was on his way back to Missouri. Upon reaching Jefferson Barracks, Grant discovered that the regiment was gone, and he would have to make haste to catch up with it. Before heading south, however, he de-termined to go to White Haven to see Julia. The prospect of a lengthy absence from her had spurred him to do something he had never thought about before. He was going to ask Julia to marry him. Grant wrote in his memoirs that he might have carried on a relationship with Julia for a long time without realizing that he had fallen in love with her, but the prospect of not seeing her again for an extended time "sud-denly developed my sentiment so palpably that there was no mistak-ing it." When Ulysses reached White Haven, he made his intentions known to Julia, and she agreed that the two would join their lives to-gether when he returned from Texas. They were engaged, but the wed-ding would have to be postponed indefinitely. It would be more than four years before the marriage would take place.

Neither family was happy with the arrangement. Colonel Dent wanted more for his daughter than could be provided on the pay of a young lieutenant, and though he liked Ulysses, he thought he was not suitable as a potential husband for his daughter. Nonetheless, he grudg-ingly gave his blessing to the union. Jesse Grant was quite another matter. He was outraged that his son had become entangled with a slave-holding family and violently protested against the engagement, vowing that he would not attend the wedding and would not accept Julia as a daughter-in-law.

Grant could not concern himself with this family squabbling for the present. He was headed for harm's way and his first taste of war. In September 1845, the 4th Infantry was transferred from Louisiana to Corpus Christi, Texas, at the mouth of the Nueces River, and Grant was with them. He received his first promotion at Corpus Christi, being advanced from the rank of brevet second lieutenant to that of a full second lieutenant. The American army, some 3,000 strong, was under the command of General Zachary Taylor. There were, as yet, no open hostilities between the United States and Mexico, and the life of the soldier in camp was dull and monotonous. Lieutenant James Longstreet tried to liven up the camp by directing plays, which were performed for the amusement of the officers and men. Grant took part in at least one of Longstreet's theatrical productions, playing a part in *Othello*.

In March 1846, General Taylor was ordered to march his army 150 miles south, to the Rio Grande, on the opposite shore from Mat-amoras, Mexico. The Mexican government was being goaded into making some sort of offensive movement against the American force, and Taylor had been ordered south in the hope that it would create an incident and touch off the war. Taylor established his base at Port Isa-bel while a portion of his force occupied Fort Texas, on the north side of the Rio Grande. On May 3, Mexican forces opened fire on the fort, and for the next five days, it was subjected to a constant bombardment. Grant was stationed at Port Isabel, some distance in the rear, but the sounds of the artillery duel could be plainly heard there. This was the first time that the young lieutenant had ever heard the din of battle. Instead of being exhilarated over the prospects of seeing action for the first time, Grant was pensive and wished that he was almost anywhere but in Texas. "I felt sorry that I had enlisted," he later wrote.

Grant's attitude was not caused by cowardice. Instead, it was based on the fact that he felt this war to be morally wrong and was embarrassed to be taking part in it. He was torn between doing his duty as an officer and following his conscience. In the end, duty won out, but it was a choice he regretted for the rest of his life. He would later write, "I had very strong opinions on the subject. I do not think there was ever waged a more wicked war than that waged by the United States on Mexico. I thought so at the time, when I was a youngster, only I had not moral courage enough to resign." Despite these feelings, "I considered my supreme duty was to my flag. I had a horror of the Mexican War, and I have always believed that it was on our part most unjust."

The Mexican army withdrew from Matamoros, but General Taylor was unable to mount an active pursuit because he was running short on supplies. Once this situation was remedied, Taylor struck out in the direction of Reynosa. On June 6, he sent part of his command that had been assembled to move quickly, called a flying column, toward Reynosa and followed with his main body. From Reynosa, Taylor determined to march on Monterrey in early September. The distance between Reynosa and Monterrey was about 100 miles, and it took the army two weeks to march it. The journey was a pleasant one, all things considered, as this portion of Mexico was rich with agricultural products. Each step the soldiers trod took them through fields of ripe vegetables and orchards of fruit-laden trees. A force of 1,000 mounted Mexican troops hovered around Taylor's army but declined to offer any resistance. For the American soldiers in the ranks, it was more like a summer lark than an active military campaign.

The lark ended when they reached Monterrey. This adobe and stone city contained 8,000 to 10,000 soldiers, commanded by General Pedro de Ampudia. Taylor's army had been reinforced, but it still numbered only 6,230 men, divided about equally between regular soldiers and volunteers. Taylor would be assuming the role of the aggressor against a superior force that was positioned behind strong fortifications. Though the Americans had artillery with them, it was of the field variety and not suitable for conducting siege operations. For their part, the Mexicans had established five strong forts within the city. Each fort was supplied with artillery, and the overall network guarded every approach to the city. Of these, the strongest were known as the Citadel, the Cathedral, and the Bishop's Palace. Taylor reconnoitered the town and determined to make his initial thrust against the Citadel, which guarded the northern approach.

On September 20, Taylor opened the Battle of Monterrey by ordering his light artillery to fire on the defenders in the Citadel. General William J. Worth was ordered to march his division on a flanking movement, to the west of the city. Taylor had received intelligence that the road leading southwest from Monterrey to Saltillo could be taken and held by the Americans. If this could be accomplished, the defenders of Monterrey would be cut off from receiving supplies or reinforcements. Taylor ordered Worth to take the road and, when that was accomplished, to mount an attack against the city from the west with his division. Worth's men succeeded in capturing the road, but the movement alerted the defenders in the Bishop's Palace, and it was deemed inadvisable to make a frontal assault against the fortifications from that direction. A desultory fire was continued against the Citadel until dark, and General David Twigg's division was ordered to make a demonstration against the works to draw attention away from Worth.

The following day, General Taylor ordered forward his three larger pieces of artillery—two 24-pound howitzers and a 10-inch mortar—and he concentrated all of his big guns against the Citadel. While the bombardment was taking place, General Worth launched an attack against the Bishop's Palace. A large force of Mexican cavalry rode out of the city to attack Worth. The Americans held their ground and soon put the troopers to flight with several well-aimed volleys, inflicting casualties of 100 killed and wounded on the attackers. Furthermore, Worth's men were able to get between the Mexican cavalrymen and Monterrey, preventing them from reentering the city.

In the meantime, Taylor had sent his infantry forward against the Citadel. The Americans were driving the defenders back and had actually entered the city, where fighting was taking place in the streets. The 4th Infantry, and Lieutenant Ulysses S. Grant, were taking an active part in this movement. Grant had been assigned as the regimental quartermaster for the 4th Infantry and had been charged with supervising the supplies that the unit needed. In this capacity, his proper place was in the rear, with the wagon train, when the regiment went into battle. Grant was indeed with the wagons when the fighting was approaching its climax in the streets of Monterrey. The fury of the firing got the better of the young lieutenant, and he turned over command of the wagons to another officer and rode to the sound of the guns. Grant rode into the city, where he found a group of Americans pinned down by a deadly fire from the Mexican defenders. The Americans were running short on ammunition, and Grant volunteered to go back and get some. His skills as a horseman were put to the test during this ride. With his arm around the horse's neck and his right foot in the left stirrup, he concealed himself on the left side of the horse's body as he rode past Mexican soldiers who fired numerous shots at him. On the outskirts of town, he came across two badly wounded American soldiers, to whom he promised to send medical assistance. Procuring the ammunition, Grant made his way back to the city, but the remnant of the force he had left was in full retreat by the time he arrived. Nonetheless, his gallantry had distinguished him in the eyes of his superiors.

Though Taylor's assault had been thrown back, Worth's division was making steady progress in their attack from the west side of the city. Fighting continued for the next two days, with Worth capturing Bishop's Palace on the 22nd. On September 23, Taylor resumed an all-out offensive against the city, as his forces inched forward in bloody house-to-house fighting. The Americans were driving the Mexican army back, and General Ampudia felt that it was just a matter of time before his army was defeated. He asked Taylor for surrender terms and was informed that he and his men would be permitted to march away, with their weapons, if he would only surrender the city to the Americans. Ampudia agreed to these terms, and the fighting for Monterrey was ended.

While Taylor's victory was heralded by most of the people at home, he got himself into a bit of trouble with the administration for allowing Ampudia's army to withdraw with their weapons. Taylor would go on to win a brilliant victory at the Battle of Buena Vista, but his theater of operations became of secondary importance following the capture

of Monterrey. The administration decided to focus its main emphasis with the army of General Winfield Scott, which had been landed
at Vera Cruz and was preparing to march inland toward Mexico City.
Most of Taylor's regulars, including the 4th Infantry, were transferred
to Scott's army. Grant had admired Taylor and felt him to be a capable
field commander. Now he would get the opportunity to observe another American military hero. Taylor seemed completely unmilitary in
his dress and deportment. He usually dressed in civilian clothes, and he
usually had few, if any, staff officers accompanying him. Scott, in contrast, always appeared in full military regalia and always looked the part
of the great soldier. He was always surrounded by a full compliment of
staff officers and delegated many of the duties that Taylor did himself.
Grant would come to admire Scott's abilities just as much as he did
Taylor's, and the contrast in styles between the two men gave different
ideas that he would incorporate in his own command structure when
he was in command of an army. Grant himself had a nature more like
Taylor than Scott. A quote from his memoirs shows that he felt closer
to Taylor. "Both were pleasant to serve under—Taylor was pleasant to
serve with."

The army General Scott gathered together before Vera Cruz numbered approximately 12,000 men. Its objective was Mexico City,
200 miles inland. The entire route to the Mexican capital would be
uphill, as Vera Cruz was at sea level and Mexico City was 11,000 feet
above sea level. Scott's men would be advancing through the heart of
the enemy's country, surrounded by more than seven million hostile
inhabitants. The mission seemed like an impossible undertaking. But
the vast majority of the Mexican citizens were peasants, living like serfs
in a feudal society, who hated their Mexican rulers more than they did
the invading Americans.

Vera Cruz was captured after a brief struggle, and the Americans
advanced steadily toward their goal, despite a number of small battles
and skirmishes that were fought along the way. Grant took no part
in any of the fighting. He was occupied with his duties as regimental
quartermaster and was usually to be found in the rear of the army with
his wagons. Grant performed his duties diligently, but his heart was not
in his work. It was during the Mexican War that he developed a taste

for liquor and began to drink heavily. A solitary individual by nature, he tended to keep his own company, despite the obvious loneliness he felt. This feeling of isolation, of not belonging, combined with his aversion for military life and his personal objections to the war he was participating in, created in Grant a need to escape from reality, and those temporary escapes were found inside of a bottle. Little notice was taken of Grant's drinking. In that time, practically everyone drank, and intoxication was not looked upon as being a personal liability unless it was taken to excess. Officer's messes were provided with alcohol, and whiskey rations were commonly given to the men in the ranks. In fact, Grant had been out of place when he did not drink. But he did not imbibe in the usual manner. He did not attend parties or gatherings, and he rarely drank in the company of others. For Grant, drinking became a solitary pursuit. It did not bring with it the gaiety or camaraderie that most of his fellow officers experienced when they partook of spirits. His drinking habits showed all the signs of becoming a problem, but in that time and era no one could read the signs.

As General Scott's army neared Mexico City, the fighting became more frequent and more severe. Pitched battles were fought at Contreras and Churubusco. At Molina del Rey, one of the bloodiest engagements of the war took place. The key point in the Mexican defenses was a long stone building that had been filled with Mexican infantrymen. The struggle for possession of this building saw the tide of battle sweep back and forth, as the structure was captured and lost several times in fierce hand-to-hand fighting. Grant had left the relative security of his supply train during this fight and had ventured forward to the front. When he reached the scene of combat, he saw Frederick Dent lying seriously wounded on the ground, right in the middle of the contending forces. Grant rescued his future brother-in-law from the melee and saved his life.

Scott's forces won the Battle of Molina del Rey and pushed forward to the very gates of the city of Mexico. Here was fought the Battle of Chapultepec, the decisive engagement of the campaign. The walls of the city provided a strong defensive position for the Mexican army, and an assault against them would surely come at a high cost in American lives. Grant, always a practical man, noticed that a church with a high steeple stood just outside of the city walls, and he quickly developed a plan to turn the Mexican defenses. He secured a howitzer from an artillery unit and gathered together a small band of volunteers to serve the cannon. The men took apart the howitzer and carried it up the stairs to the steeple in pieces. There they reassembled it and opened fire on the Mexican defenders within the walls. The fire from Grant's lone gun did a great deal of damage to the enemy works and was responsible for inflicting a large number of casualties. Grant could not believe that the Mexicans did not challenge his position. "Why they did not send out a small party to capture us, I do not know. We had no infantry or other defenses besides our one gun." General Worth noticed the effects of the firing and was so impressed by the daring and initiative Grant had shown that he sent one of his staff officers to compliment him and bring him back for a personal interview. Lieutenant John C. Pemberton was the subordinate Worth selected to carry his personal congratulations to Grant. Pemberton would witness the effects of Grant's artillery again 16 years later when he was the Confederate commander of Vicksburg, Mississippi.

On September 14, 1847, the Mexican army surrendered, and the American forces entered the city as conquerors. The peace treaty that was drawn up was exceedingly harsh on the Mexicans. It stipulated that Mexico would renounce all claim to any land north of the Rio Grande, including Texas, California, Arizona, and New Mexico. Mexico lost about half of its total territorial possessions as a result of this treaty, for which it was paid the sum of $15 million by the U.S. government.

The American army became an occupation force. With the hostilities ended, most of the officers and men occupied their free time exploring the country as tourists. Grant took part in some sightseeing excursions, and he even went to a bullfight. To an animal lover like Grant, the spectacle in the arena was barbaric. "The sight to me was sickening," he wrote. "I could not see how human beings could enjoy the sufferings of beasts, and often of men, as they seemed to do on these occasions." A short time of watching the matadors plying their craft was enough to show him that this was not the sort of entertainment he could enjoy. When a horse was gored to death in the ring, he had seen enough. "I confess that I felt sorry to see the cruelty to the bull and the horse. I did not stay for the conclusion of the performance; but while I did stay there was not a bull killed in the prescribed manner."

Grant was not one to socialize to any great extent, and sightseeing held no special interest for him, so what could he do with his free time in Mexico City? He rented a bakery and went into business to benefit the regimental fund. The bakery was a huge success, and the chief commissary of the army even gave him a contract to provide bread for the troops. "In two months I made more money for the fund than my pay amounted to during the entire war." Grant seemed to be a natural businessman, and he enjoyed running a successful enterprise. This would be the only successful business venture he would enter into during his entire life.

Chapter 4

RETURN TO CIVILIAN LIFE

In the summer of 1848, Grant returned from Mexico, and his wartime adventure was ended. A four-month leave of absence was granted to the young lieutenant to go home. Grant brought two things back with him from Mexico: a new horse and a servant named Gregory. Both would soon be gone. The horse ended up being raffled off, and Gregory returned to Mexico within the year. His overriding thought was of Julia, and preparations were made for the wedding that had been almost four years in coming to pass. Grant took time to reflect on his first experience with war, however. He thought it was "of great advantage to me afterwards. Besides the many practical lessons it taught, the war brought nearly all of the officers of the regular army together so as to make them personally acquainted. It also brought them in contact with volunteers, many of whom served in the rebellion afterwards."

Grant went to St. Louis by way of Bethel, Ohio, stopping for a visit with his family. When the stagecoach pulled into town, his family saw Grant attentively help a lady with her luggage. "They all thought as much as could be that it was Julia that I had brought home." The family was mistaken. It was not Julia; Ulysses was just being a gentleman to a woman with whom he had shared the coach. After spending some time with his parents and siblings, he was off for St. Louis and Julia. His family did not go with him. Jesse had vowed that he would not attend a marriage between his son and the daughter of slave owners, and he meant to keep that promise.

Julia and Ulysses were married on August 22, 1848. In attendance were members of the Dent family and a few friends, including James P. Longstreet, who served as an attendant for Grant. Longstreet and Grant had become friends in Mexico. A quiet and introspective individual, Longstreet possessed many of the same character traits as Grant and was to become the closest friend he would have in the years before the Civil War. Julia and Grant's honeymoon consisted of a leisurely trip down the Mississippi River and up the Ohio. This was Julia's first time away from St. Louis, and the trip must have been an adventure for her. When the happy couple reached Louisville, they paid a visit to two of Grant's cousins and their families. Solomon Grant and James Hewitt were both wealthy businessmen who were well connected throughout the country. Grant had told Julia that he might resign his commission if either of these relatives were willing to offer him a job, but that offer was not forthcoming. Neither cousin even offered to introduce him to one of their many contacts. Grant would remain in the army. He and Julia would make do with a lieutenant's pay for the time being.

From Louisville, the newlyweds traveled to Bethel for a six-week visit with Grant's family. Despite Jesse's objection over his son's choice for a wife, it appears that he welcomed his new daughter-in-law cordially. Grant's brothers and sisters made her feel welcome, but it was his mother, Hannah, with whom Julia developed the fondest bond. Julia described her as being the "sweetest, kindest woman I ever met, except my own dear mother." By October 1848, Grant's leave was almost used up, and the couple returned to St. Louis to make arrangements for his next posting. He had been ordered to report to Detroit. Colonel Dent did not want to see his daughter become an army wife at a desolate post. He did not have the means to set Ulysses up in business and persuade him to leave the army, however. The couple was married; there was nothing he could do about that now, but he did not intend to let Julia waste her life following her husband from post to post across the country. He proposed that Grant report to Detroit while Julia remained at White Haven. She could remain in a stable, comfortable environment, and he could visit her during his leaves, once or twice a year. The suggestion was preposterous, but it made all the sense in the world to Colonel Dent. Julia broke into tears as her father described his plan, and Grant asked if she would prefer to stay at White Haven. Through her tears, she told him no, and the question was settled. The couple would face whatever the army sent its way together.

The couple made the arduous journey to Detroit, only to be informed that Grant's orders had been changed. He was now to report to Sackett's Harbor in New York, on the eastern shore of Lake Ontario. Ulysses filed an official protest of the change of orders and requested a reinstatement of the original destination, but he and Julia dutifully made arrangements to proceed to New York. They arrived at the remote post just in time for a Great Lakes winter and set up housekeeping. The Grants interacted enjoyably with the other officers and wives on the post, and Sackett's Harbor would prove to be one of the happiest places they would live during their lives together.

It was a new beginning for the happy young couple, and married life seemed to suit them well. Grant made a new beginning of his own while at Sackett's Harbor. A new husband with new responsibilities, he decided it was time to deal with the drinking problem he had acquired during the Mexican War. Grant joined the Temperance League and became one of the organizers of a chapter at the post. He recognized that he had a drinking problem and wanted to take steps to correct it. For the time being, at least, he was on the wagon and had taken a vow of sobriety.

In the spring of 1849, Grant was transferred to Detroit, where the 4th Infantry had its headquarters. Ulysses was to perform the duties of the regimental quartermaster. The couple rented a small house near the post and set about establishing their second home in the army. Grant had little to do in the quartermaster's department. One of his enlisted men was an extremely efficient clerk and took care of virtually all of the duties of the quartermaster himself. This left Grant with a great deal of free time, as well as a great amount of boredom. The pledge of sobriety he had taken in Sackett's Harbor was soon forgotten, as he drank to fill the idle hours.

While the Grants were living in Detroit, the state ratified a new constitution, which granted Michigan citizenship to any U.S. citizen who was then living within its borders. Zachariah Chandler was running for mayor of Detroit, and all of the army personnel at the post were encouraged to cast their votes in the election. Grant declined to vote. He was from Ohio, and "I did not wish to consider myself a citizen of Michigan."

Ulysses and Julia spent two years in Detroit. Their first child, Frederick Dent Grant, was born on May 30, 1850. The couple was not together at the time of the birth. Julia had returned to St. Louis, and her father's home, prior to the delivery to be in more comfortable surroundings. Grant would have to wait for months to see his son, as Julia did not return to Detroit until the fall of that same year. While Julia was gone, Grant rented a small cottage with another officer in an attempt to save what little money he could from his army pay.

In the spring of 1851, the 4th U.S. Infantry was ordered to Sackett's Harbor. This must have been a sort of homecoming for the Grants, though it was to be short in duration. In the spring of 1852, the regiment was ordered to the Pacific coast. This new assignment would cause the second separation for the Grants in as many years. Julia was pregnant with the couple's second child, and Ulysses felt that the arduous trip would place too much strain on her delicate condition. It was decided that she would stay with her family until after the baby was born and would follow him when the right opportunity presented itself. Ulysses S. Grant Jr. was born on July 22, 1852. Grant did not receive word of the birth for some time. On July 5, the 4th Infantry had boarded ships in New York Harbor, bound for Panama. The regiment reached Panama on July 16, but problems with transportation, and a cholera epidemic, caused a six-week delay before it could complete the final leg of its journey to California. By the end of August, the 4th Infantry was finally prepared to leave Panama. One out of every seven had fallen victim to cholera, however, and were left behind in Panamanian graves. Grant and his comrades reached San Francisco in early September and took in all the sights of the raucous, bustling gold-boom town. After a four-week stay at Benicia Barracks, the regiment was ordered to Fort Vancouver, on the Columbia River.

The great influx of people into the gold camps and mining towns had caused inflated prices for consumer goods that made living in the region a very expensive undertaking. Grant reported, "A cook could not be hired for the pay of a captain," and stated that "it would have been impossible for officers of the army to exist upon their pay, if it had not been that authority was given them to purchase from the commissary such supplies as he kept, at New Orleans wholesale prices." While at Vancouver, Grant and three other officers decided to put a large tract of land under cultivation and raise potatoes. The crop would augment their own scant rations, and the surplus could be sold at a handsome profit. A flood of the Columbia River in June killed most of the crop and ruined this business venture. Grant, ever pragmatic, said, "This saved digging it up, for everybody on the Pacific coast seemed to have come to the conclusion at the same time that agriculture would be profitable. In 1853 more than three-quarters of the potatoes raised were permitted to rot in the ground, or had to be thrown away."

In August 1853, Grant was promoted to the rank of captain and given command of a company stationed at Fort Humboldt. He and Julia had been apart for more than a year at this point, and Ulysses had already begun to sink into the pits of despair and boredom. His drinking became habitual, and he was a constant visitor at a local tavern in Eureka. Grant's regimental commander, Colonel Robert Buchanan, took notice of his subordinate's frequent intoxication and slovenly appearance and wondered if Grant was a poor fit for the army. Grant himself probably agreed with Buchanan's assessment. He had never aspired to a military career and was dreadfully homesick for Julia and his family. In his memoirs, Grant simply states that his pay as a captain was insufficient to support his wife and family, so "I concluded, therefore, to resign." In this explanation, he declined to comment on the part his drinking had in bringing about his resignation. Colonel Buchanan had discussed Grant's drinking habits with him, at which time the captain wrote out his resignation. Grant promised to stop drinking and asked that the resignation not be forwarded to the War Department so long as he kept sober. This latest sobriety pledge was short-lived, and a public exhibition of drunkenness caused Colonel Buchanan to execute the resignation he had been holding on July 31, 1854. Grant was out of the army. Penniless, and without any prospects for earning a living, he would have to return to his family in disgrace.

His journey home from Fort Humboldt shows clearly how destitute Grant's fortunes had become. A comrade in the Quartermaster's

Department in San Francisco loaned him the money to secure transportation to New York City. When he arrived there, he had used up practically all of the money he had borrowed and found himself stranded in the city. His father had promised to send him money to buy a railroad ticket to Bethel, but that had not arrived. Without means to provide for his own existence, Grant went to see an old classmate from West Point, Captain Simon B. Buckner, who was on detached duty as a recruiting officer in the city. Buckner gave Grant enough funds to pay for food and lodging while he waited for his father's money to arrive.

When he finally made his way to Bethel, Ulysses received a stern welcome from his disappointed father. Jesse Grant had already written to Jefferson Davis, secretary of war, asking him to take his son back in the army and stating that his many years of soldier life had made him "poorly suited for the pursuits of private life." His appeal failed to bring about the desired result. His son's resignation had already been filed, and the case was closed.

Ulysses traveled on to St. Louis, where he was reunited with Julia for the first time in two years. It would be the first time that he had ever gotten to see his second son, Ulysses Jr. Colonel Dent did what he could to help his daughter and her family. He gave 80 acres of ground to the couple to start a farm, which Grant appropriately named Hardscrabble. There was no house on the property, so Grant and the family were forced to live with the Dents until one could be built. In the meantime, Colonel Dent had offered Ulysses employment as an overseer on his estate. An ex-captain of infantry should have been an excellent candidate for such a position, but Grant proved to be a total failure at the undertaking. He was far too soft with the servants and made pets out of all of the livestock.

Grant devoted all of his energies to farming and tried to make a living from tilling the soil. With the help of friends and neighbors, he constructed a log cabin on the property for he and his family to live in, and he cut and sold firewood to earn spending money while waiting for his crop to come in. On July 4, 1855, a third child was born: Ellen "Nellie" Grant. Ulysses's family was growing, even if his prospects were not. For four years, he toiled on the farm without being able to make it profitable. In the course of those four years, his father had loaned him $2,000, an exorbitant amount of money for the time. By 1858, there was no denying that the farm was a losing proposition, and Grant was forced to sell his livestock and farming implements at auction. The money raised by the auction paid off a few of his many debts but fell far short of relieving his financial dilemma. Julia had given birth to their fourth child, Jesse Root Grant, on February 6 of that year, and Grant was now faced with the problem of supporting a family of six with no money, no job, and no prospects. Indeed, his financial situation was worse than it had been when he resigned from the army.

In January 1859, Colonel Dent persuaded a friend in St. Louis to take his son-in-law on as a partner in his business. Henry Boggs owned a real estate agency in the city, and Colonel Dent convinced him that Ulysses's familiarity with the people of the area would make him an asset to the business. Boggs reluctantly agreed to give Grant a try, and Boggs & Grant went into business on New Year's Day. Grant's shy and retiring personality was completely unsuited for the real estate business, and Boggs was quick to see that he had made a mistake in taking him into the firm. By the fall of that same year, Boggs dissolved the partnership and terminated Grant's affiliation with the firm. He was once more without a job, and it looked for all the world as if he might end his days as a penniless and pathetic individual. Julia owned two slaves, and Grant tried to sell them, or hire them out, as a means of obtaining money to support his family. Much to his chagrin, he found that there were no takers to buy or hire the servants. He was in the depths of despair when he borrowed money to visit his father and ask for his assistance.

Jesse had set Ulysses's two younger brothers, Orvil and Simpson, up in the leather business in Galena, Illinois. The brothers had established the business as a thriving enterprise, and Jesse thought that they might be able to take Ulysses on as an assistant. The situation was far from being desirable. Orvil and Simpson looked upon Ulysses as a charity case and felt as if they were carrying their failure of an older brother. Ulysses was humiliated to be placed in the position of being a ward of his younger brothers and hated the idea of working in the tannery as much as he ever had. Still, it was the only offer of employment he had, and the salary of $800 a year must have seemed like a fortune during those tough and trying times. Grant consented to accept the position and became a clerk in his brother's store. By all accounts, he was not a very good clerk. He did not have a business mind and was not successful at being a salesman. When any important customer entered the shop, one of his brothers would invariably push him out of the way and conduct the transaction himself. Grant was ashamed of the circumstances to which he had fallen. In his despair and depression, he shut himself off from the outside world. During his time in Galena, he made no friends and precious few acquaintances. Though he had a job and was making an honest living for himself and his family, he must have felt as if he had sunk as low as a man could sink. At 37 years of age, the cares and labors of life had already caused him to walk with a broken and slouched posture, and the appearance of his face had become aged far beyond his years. The future seemed as dark as the present. There was nothing on the horizon to promise any rescue from his dire existence, and he might have spent all of his remaining days as a nondescript employee in Galena. But war clouds were forming across the nation, and though he could not know it at the time, the coming conflict would restore him to army life and propel him to national prominence.

Chapter 5

A CALL TO ARMS

The year of 1859 had witnessed growing tensions between the North and South. John Brown's raid on Harpers Ferry, Virginia, had been intended as the start of a slave insurrection in the South that would wash away the institution of slavery, as well as those who propagated it, in one fell swoop. Many in the North had proclaimed Brown to be a hero, and when he was executed for crimes against the nation, he was widely hailed as a martyr in the cause of abolition. The attitudes of the people in the North were viewed with fear and apprehension by those living south of the Mason-Dixon Line. Southerners felt like their Northern brethren were trying to incite a slave revolt, as if they were urging the slaves to rise up and kill their masters and destroy forever the institution that kept them in bondage. The presidential election of 1860 only added to the distrust with which the South already viewed the North. Abraham Lincoln had won the nomination of the recently formed Republican Party and would be their candidate for the presidency. The Republicans were strongly tied to the abolitionist movement in the North, and most Southerners felt Lincoln's election would place their region of the country at a severe disadvantage in national politics, relegating the Southern states to a second-class citizenship within the

Union. Lincoln won the election, despite the fact that he did not get a single electoral vote from any of the Southern or border states. Southerners viewed the results of the election as proof positive that they were soon to be relegated to a subservient role in the affairs of their own nation, and one by one, the various Southern states resolved to leave the Union and establish a government of their own.

South Carolina seceded from the Union on December 20, 1860, closely followed by Mississippi, Florida, Alabama, and Georgia. By February 1861, seven states had left the Union, and their representatives met in Montgomery, Alabama, to form the Confederate States of America. Jefferson Davis was elected president of the newly formed nation, and Montgomery was chosen to be its capital. The prevailing sentiment in the North was to allow the disaffected states of the South to leave the Union in peace, and the permanent division of the country might have taken place were it not for an incident that took place in Charleston Harbor, South Carolina. A detachment of Federal soldiers, under the command of Major Robert Anderson, had been assigned to garrison Federal military positions in Charleston. Major Anderson had a force of only 127 officers and men with which to carry out his mission, and he decided to move his whole command to Fort Sumter, an unfinished masonry fortification built in the middle of Charleston Harbor. The state officials of South Carolina were outraged by the presence of Union soldiers within their borders. They alleged that the Federal government held no claim to any property inside the boundaries of the state, as it had seceded from the Union and was no longer a part of the United States. Confederate commissioners attempted to negotiate a peaceful resolution to the problem by offering monetary compensation to the government in Washington to pay for the contended sites. The Lincoln administration would not budge. Instead of relinquishing its claims to ownership of the military sites in Charleston, the Federal government took steps to reinforce Anderson's command and strengthen its hold on the fort. When Southern leaders learned of Washington's intentions, they determined that their only course of action was to take the fort by force of arms. Accordingly, in the predawn hours of April 12, 1861, Confederate artillery opened fire on Fort Sumter. Anderson and his men were outgunned, outmanned, and surrounded. His ammunition and supplies were very low, and under the current circumstances, he had few options to consider. On April 12, he surrendered himself and his garrison and hauled down the American flag. The South had won this argument, but it had set in motion a series of events that would plunge the nation into a tragic and bloody civil war.

Public sentiment in the North changed immediately after the firing on Fort Sumter. The people were filled with wrath and indignation, and people who only the day before had been willing to allow the Confederate states to go in peace now called for vengeance over this outrage to the flag. President Lincoln made a call for 75,000 volunteers to restore the Union and put down what he now referred to as a rebellion. Up to this point, four Southern states had remained in the Union: Virginia, North Carolina, Tennessee, and Arkansas. Lincoln's call for the states to provide men from their militias to invade the Confederate states caused the legislatures of each of these states to question where their loyalty lay. They had desired to remain in the Union, but they would not take part in a military action against their sister states in an effort to coerce them back into the Union. All four states would eventually secede and cast their lot with the Confederacy.

Both sides hurriedly prepared for the war they knew was coming. Both sides felt that the entire question would be settled before the summer was ended, and each thought that its side would emerge victorious. Most young men had grown up hearing the thrilling stories of the Revolutionary War. They viewed the coming conflict as the one great chance in their lifetime for adventure and glory, and few wanted to miss the opportunity. Lincoln's quota of troops was quickly raised, and many more disappointed young men were turned away from the recruiting centers. This massive influx of volunteer soldiers also required a large number of officers to train and lead them. Men with prior military training were in high demand, especially former officers who were West Point graduates.

On April 18, 1861, Lincoln's call for volunteers reached Galena, Illinois. Posters were hung around the town for a public meeting to be held at the courthouse later that evening. The citizens of Galena packed the courthouse, and the first order of business was to choose someone to preside over the meeting that was about to take place. Grant was selected to act in this capacity, even though he was "a comparative stranger" to most of the men in attendance. Grant felt that he had been selected because "I had been in the army and seen service." Several patriotic speeches were made, and a call was made to form a company of soldiers from the town. Grant was offered the command of the company, but he declined to accept. He told them, "I would aid the company in every way I could and would be found in the service in some position if there should be a war." From that moment on, Grant's thoughts were focused on military matters. He never went back to his brother's business again. When the company left Galena for Springfield, a few days later, he went with it.

Grant planned to remain in Springfield only until the Galena Company was assigned to a regiment. When it was accepted to form part of the 11th Illinois Infantry, he thought his work was done and made plans to return to Galena. Governor Richard Yates approached Grant and asked if he would remain in the city for one more day and meet with him in his office the following morning. Grant agreed. Yates asked him to accept a position with the state's adjutant general's office, where his prior military service could be put to good use. Grant was no administrator, but he was well versed in the military way of doing things. He had served as "quartermaster, commissary and adjutant in the field. The army forms were familiar to me and I could direct how they should be made out." As for the overall management of the office, Grant acknowledged that he had shortcomings, stating, "There was a clerk in the office of the Adjutant General who supplied my deficiencies."

The duty of mustering the volunteer regiments into the service of the state fell under the responsibilities of the adjutant general's office, and Grant personally attended to the mustering of several of them. One such regiment had been given orders to assemble 18 miles southeast of St. Louis. It would take the various companies several days to reach their destination, so Grant decided to pay a visit to the Dents and combine business with pleasure. St. Louis was, at this time, a very divided city. Southern sentiments were strong with a large portion of the population, and for the moment, Unionists seemed to be on the defensive. The Missouri State Militia was camped just outside of the city and was known to be in sympathy with the South. Governor Claiborne Jackson planned for the militia to seize the U.S. arsenal in preparation for Missouri casting its lot with the Confederacy. A small Union garrison of only two companies, under the command of Captain Nathaniel Lyons, was all that stood between the militia and the cache of arms contained within the arsenal.

Francis P. Blair was a Union leader in Missouri, and he took it upon himself to raise a regiment of loyal men, which he took command of as its colonel. As tensions were reaching a breaking point, and it seemed as if the militia's capture of the arsenal was a foregone conclusion, Blair marched his force to that place and placed himself and his regiment under Lyons's command. Rumors circulated through the town that Lyons planned to turn the tables on the Southerners by marching out to Camp Jackson to capture them. Grant had known Lyons at West Point, as well as in the army afterward. On the morning of May 10, 1861, he went to the arsenal. When he got there, Lyons and Blair were forming their men for a march to Camp Jackson. Grant had never met Blair before. He introduced himself and "expressed my sympathy with his purpose." The militia surrendered without a fight, and the prisoners were marched back to the arsenal. Grant was on hand to witness the scene and to offer his congratulations to Lyons and Blair. The following day, he left St. Louis for Mattoon, Illinois, where he presided over the mustering of the 21st Illinois Regiment, a unit that he would soon have a close affiliation with.

Grant returned to Springfield, where he met with Brigadier General John Pope, who was serving as a U.S. mustering officer in the city. Grant had known Pope for three years at West Point and had served with him in the Mexican War. Pope offered to use what influence he could to secure a position for Grant in the U.S. Army, but Grant declined. He did not think he needed an "endorsement for permission to fight for my country."

Taking a short leave from the duties he was performing for Governor Yates, Grant returned home to Galena to see his family for a couple days. He took the opportunity to write a letter to General Lorenzo Thomas, adjutant general of the U.S. Army. Grant informed Thomas of his previous military service and asked that he be considered to command a regiment. "I felt some hesitation in suggesting rank as high as the colonelcy of a regiment, feeling somewhat doubtful whether I would be equal to the position. But I had seen nearly every colonel who had been mustered in from the State of Illinois, and some from

Indiana, and felt that if they could command a regiment properly, and with credit, I could also."

Grant never received a response from Thomas. He next made a trip to Cincinnati to see George B. McClellan. McClellan had recently been made a major general and given command of all Federal troops in Ohio. The two had spent a year together at West Point, and Grant was hoping that McClellan might remember him and assign him to a staff position at his headquarters. Though he called at McClellan's headquarters for two days, he failed to gain an interview with the commander and was forced to return to Springfield without a commission or a command. He did not know it at the time, but fate had decided that there would be a regiment waiting for him when he arrived in the city.

Simon B. Goode had been the elected colonel of the 21st Illinois when Grant had mustered it into state service at Mattoon. Goode soon proved himself to be incompetent to the men under his command. A committee of officers from the 21st went to see Governor Yates to lay the matter before him and to inform him they all intended to resign if a better commander could not be found for the regiment. After a short deliberation, Yates decided that Grant should have the position. On June 15, 1861, Grant assumed command at the fairgrounds, at Springfield. Colonel Goode had failed to instill any amount of military discipline in the men. They were unruly and disrespectful, especially when they got the opportunity to see their new colonel for the first time. Grant appeared in camp looking more like a vagabond than the commander of a regiment. He wore civilian clothes, donning a tattered hat and a coat that was worn through at the elbows. He was nothing like what the men envisioned when they thought about a colonel, and they began to make fun of Grant as he walked among them. One of the enlisted men got behind the colonel and was making mocking gestures when another soldier pushed him into the colonel. It was not a good beginning, but in the course of a week, "by the application of a little regular army punishment all were reduced to as good discipline as one could ask."

Grant's appearance was a source of embarrassment for several weeks following his taking command of the regiment. He did not own a uniform or a horse and did not have the money to buy either. When the regiment was turned out for dress parades, his lieutenant colonel had to assume command because of Grant's lack of a uniform. At length, a Galena businessman, E. A. Collins, forwarded the money to purchase the necessary articles, and the new colonel was able to present himself before his men in proper attire.

The regiment remained in Springfield until July 3, when it was ordered to Quincy, Illinois. Though there was a rail line between Springfield and Quincy, Grant decided to march the men to their destination as a continuation of their training. By the time the regiment crossed the Illinois River, a message came changing its objective. Grant was to hold where he was and wait for a steamer that would take the 21st to St. Louis. While the troops waited for the boat, news came that an Illinois regiment had been surrounded by Confederates at Monroe, Missouri, and Grant was given orders to take his regiment to their relief as soon as possible. The regiment was loaded on train cars and taken to Quincy, where it disembarked and prepared to cross the Mississippi River into Missouri. It appeared as if this would be the first battle the 21st Illinois would participate in, and Grant began to have second thoughts about being in command. He was a West Point graduate, to be sure, and had served honorably in the Mexican War. But he had never led men into combat. He had been assigned to the quartermaster's department in Mexico and was not a line officer. Though he had taken part in several skirmishes and battles, it had been on a volunteer basis, never as an assigned commander. As the train neared Quincy, Grant wondered if he was truly qualified for the colonelcy he had sought and questioned if he possessed the attributes of leadership necessary to lead men in a desperate struggle. His misgivings proved to be untimely, however, as no fight took place. The members of the trapped Illinois regiment straggled into Quincy just as the 21st was preparing to cross the river and go to their aid. The Confederate units that had surrounded the Illinois men withdrew when they learned that Grant's relief column was approaching, and a battle was avoided.

The regiment went to Palmyra, Illinois, and a few days later traveled on to Salt River, where it guarded workmen who were rebuilding a bridge over the Mississippi. The bridge construction took about two weeks, and when it was completed, Grant was given orders to cross into Missouri and make his way to the town of Florida, some 25 miles south. Colonel Thomas Harris, of the Missouri State Guard, was supposed to be near the town with a Confederate force, and Grant was directed to attack them. The same uneasiness that had surfaced in Quincy began to torment Grant again as his regiment neared Florida. When the reached the site of the Confederate encampment, it was discovered that Harris and his men had retreated. "It occurred to me at once that Harris had been as much afraid of me as I had been of him," Grant would later write, stating that it was a lesson "I never forgot afterwards. From that event to the close of the war, I never experienced trepidation upon confronting an enemy, though I always felt more or less anxiety, I never forgot that he had as much reason to fear my forces as I had his." He had still not led his men into battle or even had a shot fired in anger, but his experience in the field had taught him a fundamental lesson that he would employ for the remainder of the war. He would never again worry about what his enemy was going to do. Instead, he would let the enemy worry what he was about to do.

Meanwhile, back in Washington, President Lincoln was handing out general's commissions at a fantastic rate. Many of them were given for political patronage, and Elihu Washburne, a congressman from Illinois, did not want to see his section of the country ignored. He submitted Grant's name for a promotion to the grade of brigadier general, and it received the approval of both the president and Congress. Actually, Washburne need not have gone to any great deal of trouble in securing a promotion for Grant. The War Department was giving special attention to any officers who had left the army and were now returning. A list of 26 such officers who were scheduled for promotion had been drafted for the president, and Grant's name appeared sixth on that list. The promotion was made official in August, and Grant, who had been apprehensive over his abilities to lead a regiment, was now in command of a brigade.

Grant's father was obviously remembering his son's recent vocational difficulties when he offered his advice: "Be careful Ulyss; you're a general now; it's a good job, don't lose it." Colonel Dent had a completely different slant on the good fortune that had recently befallen his son-in-law. Being of Southern sympathies, Colonel Dent had been mortified when Grant entered the Union army in the first place. Now he was to become a general, leading men whom the colonel considered to be enemies of his people. "Don't talk to me about this Federal son-in-law of mine," he was reported to have said to a friend. "There shall always be a plate on my table for Julia, but none for him." The Civil War was dividing the nation in two. It was also causing splits in many families, and Grant's would be among them.

Chapter 6

OPERATIONS IN THE WEST

Grant established his headquarters at Cairo, Illinois. He was under the direct command of Major General John C. Fremont, in whose Department of the Missouri Grant's district was located. Fremont was already a famous man before the war. He had been an esteemed army officer, an explorer, an Indian fighter, and in 1856, he became the first Republican nominee to run for the presidency. Fremont made his headquarters in St. Louis and ran his department as if he was the sovereign of an independent nation. He was showy and ostentatious and relished being in the spotlight. Fremont and his new brigadier general could not have been more different.

The first task that Grant undertook upon being promoted was to gather together a staff. He chose Lieutenant C. B. Lagow, from the 21st Illinois, to serve as his aide. William S. Hillyer, a lawyer from St. Louis he had become acquainted with while living there, was also asked to join the team. Grant felt that he should also select a man from his new hometown: Galena. John A. Rawlins was also a lawyer and had been a Douglas Democrat in the recent election. But Rawlins had remained loyal to the Union, and Grant remembered him as being one of the finest public speakers he had ever heard. He offered Rawlins the rank of captain and the position of assistant adjutant general on his staff. Rawlins was just about to muster in to the service as a major with a new regiment that was being organized, but he chose to accept Grant's offer instead. Neither Lagow nor Hillyer displayed any capabilities as staff officers, and both would be gone by the end of the war. Rawlins, on the other hand, proved to be a capable and trusted assistant and would remain with Grant for the rest of his life.

The brigade spent a short period of time at Irontown before being ordered to Jefferson City to protect the central portion of Missouri from General Sterling Price and his Missouri Confederates. Grant was charged with overseeing the removal of all funds from banks in Jefferson City and the surrounding area for transport to St. Louis. With Price's Rebel army located so near, it was feared that the money might be captured. Grant had issued orders to his subordinate commanders to carry out this mission, but the operation had not yet been initiated on August 28 when he received orders to turn over his command to Colonel Jefferson C. Davis and report to headquarters in St. Louis.

General Fremont assigned Grant to command the district of south-east Missouri. This meant that all of Missouri south of St. Louis, as well as southern Illinois, would fall under his sphere of influence. Fremont was trying to drive all of the Confederate forces out of Missouri. He feared that the South would send reinforcements across the Mississippi River, from Kentucky, and Grant was charged with the task of keeping them from doing so. He established his headquarters at Cairo, Illinois, and prepared to execute his portion of Fremont's overall strategy. The Confederate forces were located about 20 miles south of Cairo, on either side of the Mississippi River. At Belmont, Missouri, there was a force of some 5,000 Confederates under the command of General Gideon Pillow. Pillow had established a camp at Belmont, surrounded by an abatis of felled trees. Across the river, on the Kentucky shore, was Fort Columbus, an earthen work containing 143 cannon. General Leonidus Polk had supervised the construction of the works as a defense for Memphis, Vicksburg, and points south. He had a heavy chain stretched across the river from the fort to Belmont in an effort to prevent Union shipping from passing the works. Fort Columbus marked the northernmost site for any Confederate fortification during the war.

Its position was thought to be strategic by both sides, as whoever controlled this area held the key to the upper Mississippi.

Grant was ordered to make a demonstration against Fort Columbus to hold the Confederates there, and at Belmont, in check and prevent them from siphoning off any of their manpower and sending them into the Missouri interior. On November 6, 1861, Grant loaded 3,000 men aboard steamers and, with an escort of two gunboats, started down the Mississippi. As the flotilla approached Belmont, Grant decided to alter his orders. Instead of merely making a demonstration, he determined to land his troops and attack the Confederates at Belmont. "I had no orders which contemplated an attack by the national troops," he would later write, "nor did I intend anything of this kind when I started out from Cairo; but after we started I saw that the officers and men were elated at the prospect of at last having the opportunity of doing what they had volunteered to do—fight the enemies of their country. I did not see how I could maintain discipline, or retain the confidence of my command, if we should return to Cairo without an effort to do something." None of the men in Grant's command had seen action thus far. The Battle of Manassas had been fought almost four months before. No great battle had yet been waged in the western theater, and the volunteers were growing restless from their months of inactivity.

Grant landed his force a few miles above Belmont and marched them toward the town. By 9:00 A.M., the Federals had made contact with Pillow's troops, and the battle was joined. Though the Confederates outnumbered the Union troops by a margin of three-to-two, Grant's men were able to push the enemy back to their camp. After a brief stand, Pillow's troops broke and ran from the field. The Union soldiers felt that they had won a great victory. They congratulated one another and speculated that the war in the West might be over. To the victor belonged the spoils, and the Union troops began ransacking the Confederate camp, looking for treasures and keepsakes. Before long, an abundant supply of whiskey made its appearance, and many of the men began drinking to their victory. Grant did what he could to stop the ransacking and restore order to his ranks. He even went so far as to order his staff officers to set fire to the camp, but it did little to dampen the celebration of the men.

The Confederates had withdrawn from the field, but they were far from being beaten. Their officers re-formed their ranks, protected by a bluff at the river's edge, and prepared for a counterattack. Two boatloads of reinforcements were sent across from Fort Columbus to aid in the effort. When the Confederates struck, they caught the scattered and disorganized Federals completely by surprise. Elation turned quickly to panic, and rumors that the Rebels had surrounded them brought the Union troops to the verge of throwing down their weapons and running for their lives. Grant had kept his head throughout, and he calmed the men by announcing that they had fought their way into the camp and "could cut our way out just as well." He restored order to the ranks, threw out skirmishers to slow down the advance of the enemy, and made his way for the boats. It was a running fight all the way, but the Federals were able to make their escape and avoid being cut off by superior numbers. Grant was the very last to board. In fact, the gangplank of the ship he got on had already been pulled up, and the paddle wheels were churning water by the time he placed his feet on the deck.

Grant's decision to engage the Confederates at Belmont had almost ended in disaster. It had been a costly venture, resulting in more than 1,200 casualties on both sides. Later in the war, Belmont would be considered little more than a skirmish, but in November 1861, it was felt to be a major battle. Grant had exceeded his orders and brought on an engagement that cost approximately 20 percent of his available force, and he might have expected some sort of disciplinary action to be taken against him. Quite the opposite was true. President Lincoln had grown impatient with his generals and had grown weary of the constant excuses he received to explain why they were not yet engaging the enemy and taking the war to the Confederates. Lincoln was delighted by Grant's initiative and fighting spirit and used him as an example to try to spur his other generals into action. Though he did not know it yet, Lincoln had found a commander with whom he shared a kindred spirit, an officer whose philosophy of war mirrored his own. Both men were practical and pragmatic. Both viewed war in mechanical terms, not in the lofty scientific manner most of Lincoln's generals approached it. War meant fighting, pure and simple, and at this early stage of the war, Lincoln had seen his armies do precious little of that.

For months, he had anxiously watched as his generals planned and prepared for battles that did not take place. The winter season was fast approaching, and both armies would soon be curtailing active operations until the spring. Grant's actions at Belmont had provided Lincoln and the country with the impression that the Union army was not idle and that positive steps were being taken to bring the Confederates to battle and end the war.

Grant had no intention of resting on his laurels. He was already planning for an offensive operation against the Confederate forces operating near his district. The Rebels had constructed a fort 35 miles up the Tennessee River from where that body empties into the Ohio River. A large, five-sided earthwork, having walls that were 20 feet high and 20 feet thick at the base, was erected to guard the Tennessee River and protect against any Union invasion using that water route. Twelve miles east of Fort Henry, the Confederates had constructed Fort Donelson, on the bank of the Cumberland River, to keep the Federals from using that route to invade Tennessee and the Deep South. Grant wanted to lead an offensive against both forts in an attempt to dislodge the Confederates and open the way to Nashville and Memphis.

General Fremont had been relieved of his department command, and Major General Henry W. Halleck had been chosen to replace him. Halleck was a man of books and theory, not a man of action. In fact, his nickname in the old army was "Brains" because of his studious nature. Grant traveled to St. Louis to lay his plan before his new commander, but he found no support from Halleck. Undaunted, Grant turned his attention to Flag Officer Andrew Foote, commander of the gunboat flotilla operating on the Mississippi River. If he could convince Foote to back his plan, the two officers might then be able to convince Halleck to give it his blessing. Foote was very receptive to Grant's argument, but it would not be the combined urgings of this naval officer and his army counterpart that would convince Halleck to allow the operation to go forward. President Lincoln had been exerting pressure on his field commanders to advance on the enemy in their respective theaters. The president had set a date of Washington's Birthday, in February, for the various commanders to have their offensives underway. Halleck did not have any plans of his own for an immediate advance against the Confederates, so he agreed to allow Grant to put his into action.

Grant was given two divisions of troops to undertake his offensive, a force of between 15,000 and 17,000 men. His division commanders were Brigadier Generals John A. McClernand and Charles F. Smith. Flag Officer Foote's four ironclad gunboats would accompany the expedition, as would three wooden gunboats (called timberclads), under the command of Lieutenant Seth L. Phelps. Transportation for the troops was quite another matter. The army could not secure enough vessels to accommodate Grant's army, so it was decided that two trips would have to be made between Cairo and the Confederate position. On February 2, the Union troops began boarding the ships to begin the invasion. Three days later, Grant's entire force was in position and ready for offensive operations.

General McClernand's division had been landed on the eastern shore of the Tennessee River, five miles above Fort Henry. General Smith's division had been landed on the western shore. McClernand's mission was to make sure the fort's garrison did not escape. Smith was to capture a small work named Fort Heiman on the Kentucky shore. The capture of this fort would virtually ensure that Fort Henry would not be able to hold out against Grant's combined military and naval forces.

Brigadier General Lloyd Tilghman was in overall command of both Forts Henry and Donelson. When he learned of Grant's approach, Tilghman knew that he had some hard decisions to make. A defense of Fort Henry would have been a difficult proposition against the force opposed to it under the best of circumstances. Tilghman was not operating under the best of conditions. Heavy rains had caused the Tennessee River to rise to the point that it had flooded the interior of the fort. Of the 17 big guns that had been mounted on Henry's walls, 8 of them were underwater, and the powder magazine had been flooded. Tilghman knew that he could not hold the fort. He directed that a detachment of artillerymen be left behind to impede the Union navy. The remainder of the garrison was ordered to make its way to Fort Donelson, where Tilghman planned to make his stand against the Union invaders.

Foote opened a bombardment against the fort on February 6. The gunboats pounded the fort for 75 minutes. Thirty-five of the 129 defenders fell as casualties to the navy's big guns. A chance shot from one of the fort's cannon struck the ironclad *Essex*, exploding the boiler and sending scalding steam through a large portion of the ship. Thirty-two sailors were killed or wounded as a result. Tilghman realized that further resistance was useless, so he surrendered the remaining 94 officers and men in his command.

Grant's expedition had been successful in achieving the first part of its mission. Fort Henry was in Union hands, and navigation of the Tennessee River was now open to Union vessels. But Grant had little to do with the capitulation of the fort. Foote's naval vessels had fought the battle, and Tilghman had actually surrendered to the navy. The men in McClernand's and Smith's divisions had taken no part in the fight. Indeed, the only real contribution of the army was in chasing the Confederate garrison as it made its way to Fort Donelson. Grant stated, "Our cavalry pursued the retreating column towards Donelson and picked up two guns and a few stragglers; but the enemy had so much the start, that the pursuing force did not get in sight of any except the stragglers." Nevertheless, the capture of Fort Henry was hailed as a great triumph in the North, and Grant received the lion's share of the recognition because he was the architect of the operation and the overall commander of the expedition.

The next order of business was the capture of Fort Donelson. Grant had telegraphed General Halleck news of his success and added, "I shall take and destroy Fort Donelson on the 8th and return to Fort Henry." Halleck was extremely cautious when it came to field operations, and he sent a message back to Grant ordering him to stay where he was, strengthen the works, and wait for reinforcements to arrive. Grant either never received the order or he willfully disobeyed it because he went forward with preparations to march his army to Donelson. The movement got underway on February 12, and the following day he had 17,000 men poised to attack the fortifications. To Halleck, Grant's actions must have seemed foolhardy. Brigadier General John B. Floyd commanded a Confederate garrison of some 20,000 men, protected by strong works and supported by heavy artillery. But Grant knew that reinforcements were on the way. Over the course of the next two days, 10,000 additional Federal troops joined Grant's army, swinging the balance of power in his favor.

Donelson had just recently been reinforced as well. On February 7, the day after Fort Henry fell, General Albert Sidney Johnston had directed that 12,000 men be sent to bolster the garrison at Fort Donelson. Johnston had wanted General Pierre G. T. Beauregard to assume command of the position. Beauregard was a West Point graduate, a career soldier, and one of the Confederacy's first heroes for his victory at the Battle of First Manassas. Beauregard was in poor health at the time, and he declined to accept the position. The responsibility for defending the fort then fell to John B. Floyd. Floyd had been President Buchanan's secretary of war and was a wanted man in the North. Charges had been made that he had betrayed his office by materially assisting the Confederacy in preparing for war against the Union.

Floyd's 17,000 men were divided into three divisions, plus a detachment of garrison troops and a unit of cavalry. The divisions were commanded by Colonel Gabriel Wharton and Generals Simon B. Buckner and Gideon J. Pillow. The fort garrison was commanded by Colonel John W. Head. Colonel Nathan Bedford Forrest commanded the cavalry.

The fort rose 100 feet above the Cumberland River, which allowed for plunging fire against any ships that tried to pass under its guns, which included ten 32-pounder smoothbores, a 6.5-inch rifled gun, and a 10-inch Columbiad. A three-mile semicircle of trenches protected the fort from the land approach and was manned by the divisions of Buckner and Pillow.

Grant had ordered his commanders not to take any action that might bring about a general engagement until his reinforcements had arrived, but a few of his subordinates launched probing attacks as soon as they arrived on the ground. On the night of February 13, a fierce winter storm brought below-zero temperatures and three inches of snow. Both sides suffered terribly from the severe cold, as few of the men had overcoats or blankets. General Floyd determined that the fort would be untenable once Grant got his entire force into position, so he called a council of war with his subordinate generals to plan a course of action. It was decided that the Confederates would try to cut their way out of the encirclement instead of waiting to be overpowered by Grant's army and Foote's gunboats. Before Floyd could put his plan into action, Foote's gunboats arrived and engaged the fort's batteries. Donelson's heavy guns responded with a bombardment that punished the Federal ships for daring to venture so near to the fort. Each of Foote's ships was struck dozens of times, and three of them were disabled. Foote himself was wounded during the attack. The gunboats were forced to break off the engagement and retire with a loss of 8 killed and 44 wounded. The Confederates did not suffer a single casualty. The failure of the gunboats convinced Grant that the army would have to capture the fort, and he began to consider the possibility of laying siege to the Confederates.

On the morning of February 15, Floyd massed Pillow's and Buckner's divisions against the Federal right flank, held by General McClernand. Pillow and Buckner were supposed to push McClernand out of the way and open an escape route for the rest of the army. McClernand's troops were pushed back, despite being reinforced by a brigade of troops from Lew Wallace's division. By 12:30 P.M., the Federals had been forced back a distance of one to two miles, and an avenue of escape had been opened.

Grant was not on the field during the fighting that morning. He had gone to confer with Flag Officer Foote, aboard his flagship, approximately three miles away. Though he was in relatively close proximity to the battle, Grant had no idea that his army was under attack. An atmospheric condition known as an acoustic shadow caused the sound waves to bounce over Grant's location, masking the musketry and artillery fire from his ears. When Grant concluded his meeting with Foote and returned to shore, he was met by several messengers from Mc-Clernand and was informed that his army had been attacked and forced to retreat. As he tried to find out the exact situation and made plans to react to the circumstances, Grant fiddled with an unlit cigar Foote had given him. At times he would hold it in his hand, and at other times, he would secure it between clenched teeth. Though Grant did not know it at the time, Floyd's actions were making a final Union victory almost a certainty.

The initial success of Pillow's and Buckner's division had led Floyd to the conclusion that the Union army had been defeated. Instead of making good his escape from the Northern encirclement, he decided to halt his forces where they were and telegraphed Richmond that he had won a great victory over the enemy. Swift action on his part would have saved his army, but Floyd decided to stand where he was and await further developments. This proved to be a fatal error. Captured Confederate prisoners were found to have three days of rations, and Grant correctly deduced that Floyd was attempting to break out of his defensive lines. He also concluded that Floyd must have massed his forces against McClernand, leaving the rest of his defensive position in a greatly weakened condition. He ordered General Smith to advance against the right of the Confederate line and found it to be thinly held. In the meantime, McClernand was reinforced, and Floyd's escape route was slammed shut. By the end of the day, Union forces had captured all of the Confederate's outer defenses, and Floyd's army was trapped.

It looked as if there was nothing to do but surrender the fort, but John B. Floyd did not intend to be taken by the Federal troops. Fearing that he would be tried and executed for treason, Floyd announced that he intended to escape from the fort. Two Confederate steamers were coming down the river and would arrive at the fort by morning. Floyd planned to take two regiments of Virginia Infantry and use the steamers to get away. The command of the garrison then fell to General Pillow, but that officer declined to accept the responsibility and made it known that he intended to go with Floyd. Simon B. Buckner was the next officer in the chain of command. Buckner was an honorable soldier, and he did not evade the responsibility. Floyd and Pillow departed on the steamers that morning, leaving Buckner and the bulk of the Confederate army to face their fate.

Later that morning, Buckner sent a message to Grant, proposing an armistice until noon and the appointment of commissioners to negotiate the "terms of capitulation." Grant had no intention of discussing terms. He responded to Buckner, stating, "Yours of this date proposing armistice, and appointment of commissioners to settle terms of capitulation is just received. No terms except an unconditional and immediate surrender can be accepted. I propose to move immediately upon your works."

Buckner reminded Grant that the fort had successfully beaten off the attack of the U.S. Navy the previous day but said he was compelled to "accept the ungenerous and unchivalrous terms which you propose." A few hours later, the Confederate command, some 15,000 men, was officially surrendered to Grant's army. Grant and Buckner had attended West Point together for three years and had served together in the old army. It was Buckner who had advanced Grant money to live on in New York City when he had resigned from the army and was trying to make his way back home. The nature of their correspondence to one another at Fort Donelson might lead one to believe that the war had severed their ties and destroyed their friendship, but such was not the case. When the two met face-to-face, Grant reported that the conversation between them was "very friendly." Buckner told him "that if he had been in command I would not have gotten up to Donelson as easily as I did. I told him that if he had been in command I should not have tried in the way I did."

The victory at Fort Donelson made Grant a national hero. In newspapers, he was called "Unconditional Surrender" Grant, and the quote "I propose to move immediately upon your works" became a national catchphrase. Reporters accompanying the army filed stories of Grant's actions during the campaign, including the incident with the cigar Foote had given him. Admirers and well-wishers assumed that the general was an avid smoker, and gifts of cigars began to flood the camp. Actually, Grant had been an infrequent smoker before Donelson. He gave away the majority of the cigars sent to him but found himself partaking of the gifts on a more frequent basis. Eventually, he gave way to the abundance of the weed and became a full-fledged cigar smoker.

Washington was quick to reward the new hero as well. A few days after the victory at Fort Donelson, Grant was promoted to the rank of major general and assigned to command of the Military Department of Western Tennessee. It would appear that his immediate superior, General Halleck, was not among his many new fans and supporters. Following the fall of Fort Donelson, Halleck had sent a congratulatory message to General David Hunter in Kansas, thanking him for his part in the campaign by way of the reinforcements he had sent to Grant's army. He also sent a message to the War Department, stating that the victory was due to the efforts of General Charles F. Smith and requesting that he be promoted to major general. Halleck never corresponded with Grant directly concerning his victory, and the closest he came to congratulating his subordinate came when a formal letter from him was published in a St. Louis newspaper thanking Flag Officer Foote, Grant, and the men under their command for their victories. Whether his actions stemmed from a conviction that Grant was not qualified, a bias over his reputation of drinking in the old army, or merely petty jealousy, Halleck embarked on a campaign to discredit and undermine his subordinate.

The capture of Forts Henry and Donelson had unhinged Albert Sidney Johnston's defensive line in the western theater. Confederate forces withdrew to Nashville, then continued south to Corinth, Mississippi. Grant had received intelligence that Johnston was retreating, and he made plans to advance his army to Nashville, which lay within his department. He had sent messages concerning his activities to his chief-of-staff, at Cairo, to be forwarded to Halleck's headquarters, keeping him apprised of his movements. But messages from Halleck were greatly delayed in reaching Grant. Part of the reason for this was that the telegraph operator at the end of the line, whose responsibility it was to forward the dispatches, was a Southern sympathizer, and he made sure Halleck's telegrams were not delivered. Unknown to Grant, orders had been sent directing him to report immediately the number of men in his army. He had also been ordered not to advance to Nashville, which he did. Halleck telegraphed General George B. McClellan, general-in-chief of all the Union armies, complaining that Grant had been neglectful and inefficient and had disregarded orders. He forwarded the suggestion that General Smith was the only officer with Grant's army who was capable of commanding such a force. He even reported that there was a rumor that Grant "has resumed his former bad habits," insinuating that the general had been drinking heavily. McClellan's response was based on Halleck's information. He told Halleck, "General must observe discipline as well as private soldiers. Do not hesitate to arrest him at once, if the good of the service requires it, and place General Smith in command."

On March 4, Grant received a scathing message from Halleck, directing him to turn his command over to General Smith and to remain at Fort Henry. "Why do you not obey my orders to report strength and positions of your command?" Halleck demanded. This was the first Grant had been informed that Halleck had requested such information, and he was dumbfounded by the entire affair. He dutifully complied with the orders and awaited further word from his superior. In the meantime, President Lincoln had become involved in the controversy. Lincoln saw Grant as a fighting general, and he did not want to lose such a man without justification. Lincoln advised that an official inquiry be made into the allegations Halleck had brought forth. Halleck must have known that an inquiry would reflect badly upon him, and he quickly backed down and assumed a conciliatory attitude toward Grant. In his correspondence with Grant, he even went so far as to declare that it was the officials in Washington who had wrongly persecuted the general and to present himself as Grant's defender and supporter against these malicious attacks. By March 13, the entire affair was dropped, and Grant was restored to command of his army. By this time, his troops had advanced to Savannah and Pittsburg Landing, Tennessee, on the Tennessee River, and Grant hurried to join them. He would resume command of the army on March 17.

Pittsburg Landing was 20 miles north of Corinth, Mississippi, where the Confederate army was concentrated. Corinth was a strategic position because the two primary railroads in the Mississippi Valley formed a junction there. As such, it was a critical transportation hub and an important supply depot for the Confederacy. If Grant could capture Corinth, he could seriously damage the enemy's ability to wage war in the Mississippi Valley. Grant's army, named the Army of the Tennessee, would be cooperating with the Army of the Ohio, commanded by Major General Don Carlos Buell, in the campaign against Corinth. This joint operation had already been in progress for a few weeks. Buell's forces had been responsible for capturing Nashville, even though the city lay within Grant's department.

The Army of the Tennessee was composed of six divisions, totaling approximately 48,000 men. The division commanders were Charles F. Smith, John A. McClernand, Stephen A. Hurlburt, William T. Sherman, Lew Wallace, and Benjamin M. Prentiss. General Smith was bedridden with a leg injury sustained from jumping into a rowboat. William H. L. Wallace was appointed to lead Smith's division until he recovered. But Smith would develop a case of chronic dysentery while he was convalescing and would die on April 25, 1862. General Buell's army numbered some 40,000 men, and when it arrived on the scene, Grant would have close to 90,000 men with which to confront the Confederates.

General Johnston's Army of Tennessee, in Corinth, numbered only about 40,000 men. It was outnumbered by Grant's Army of the Tennessee even before Buell's forces were added to the equation. By the time the two Union armies combined, the Confederates would be facing an enemy with more than a two-to-one advantage in manpower. Corinth had been converted into a fortified town, with a line of strong works encircling it, but Johnston felt that it could not be held against the Union's overwhelming numbers and superior artillery. If he waited for Grant and Buell to join forces, he would be trapped in Corinth and the tragedies of Forts Henry and Donelson might be repeated. Therefore, Johnston determined to seize the initiative and take the fight to the enemy before their forces were joined. If he could defeat Grant and cripple the Army of the Tennessee, he could then face Buell's army on somewhat even terms. If he could fight the Union armies one at a time, there was still a chance for victory. His chances of success were small, to be sure, but Johnston had few good options available to him. On April 3, 1862, Johnston marched his army north from Corinth, hoping to surprise the Federals at Pittsburg Landing. His four corps were commanded by Generals Braxton Bragg, William J. Hardee, Leonidus Polk, and John C. Breckinridge.

The bulk of Grant's army was located just south of Pittsburg Landing, on the western bank of the Tennessee River. Bases were established on the river 5 miles north, at Crump's Landing, on the western bank and 10 miles north, at Savannah, on the eastern bank. The base at Savannah was the place where Grant anticipated the arrival of Buell's Army of the Ohio and was held by a large detachment of men. Crump's Landing was held by Lew Wallace's entire division. This meant that the main body of the Army of the Tennessee, just south of Pittsburg Landing, had approximately 33,000 men and was inferior in strength to the army Albert Sidney Johnston was marching north to attack it.

Poor roads and rainy spring weather caused Johnston's army to make a slow and toilsome march to Pittsburg Landing. It would take four days for the Confederates to cover the 20 miles that separated the opposing armies, and Southern leaders were convinced that this lack of celerity would alert the Union army to their approach and eliminate any chance to surprise the enemy. However, Grant at this time seems to have been so completely focused on mounting an offensive himself that he shunned any ideas that the Confederates might place him on the defensive by attacking his position. Various reports had come in to headquarters concerning Confederate activity and warning of enemy massing in front of Pittsburg Landing, but Grant refused to believe that his army was in danger. General Sherman, in immediate command of the forces around Pittsburg Landing, echoed his superior's sentiments. Grant and Sherman were so convinced that Johnston would not dare to attack them that they failed to order the construction of fieldworks in front of the Union lines and did not post sufficient pickets to guard the position and give warning of an impending attack. In addition, Grant spent every night at Savannah, 10 miles away, where he awaited the approaching vanguard of Buell's army.

On the night of April 5, Grant telegraphed Halleck, "I have scarcely the faintest idea of an attack being made upon us" but said that he would be ready for it if one materialized. His lack of preparedness shows that his mind-set was entirely against the probability that such an attack would be made. For Sherman's part, an Ohio colonel reported that there was a great deal of enemy activity in his front and warned that an attack upon the Union camp was imminent. Sherman became outraged by the colonel's warning and yelled, "Take your damned regiment back to Ohio. There is no enemy nearer than Corinth." General Buell arrived at Savannah on the evening of April 5, along with General William Nelson's division. The rest of the Army of the Ohio was strung out in a line of march from Savannah to Nashville and would be arriving over the course of the next couple days. As Savannah was on the eastern bank of the Tennessee River, transportation would have to be provided to get Nelson's men across to join Grant's army.

But General Johnston did not intend to wait for Nelson's reinforcement to get across the river. On the night of April 5, he put the finishing touches to his plan to defeat the Federal army in his front. His four corps were ordered to attack in stacked lines of battle. General William Hardee's corps would form the first line of battle. Behind it would be the corps of Braxton Bragg. The third line would serve as the army reserve and would be made up of General Leonidus Polk's corps and a portion of John C. Breckinridge's corps. Johnston had instructed his commanders that "every effort should be made to turn the left flank of the enemy, so as to cut off his line of retreat to the Tennessee River and throw him back on Owl Creek, where he will be obliged to surrender." Owl Creek formed an expanse of marshy land to the north of the right flank of the Union army. If the Confederates could drive the Federals into this swamp, they would force them away from their protective gunboats and keep them separated from any force Buell might be able to get across the river.

In the early morning hours of April 6, Hardee's line went forward to initiate the battle. On the Federal side, the troops were blissfully ignorant of the horror that would soon be unleashed on them. Some were up and preparing breakfast, and some were still sleeping in their tents. General Prentiss's division was camped on the front line of the Union position. Sherman's camps extended his line to the right. Mc-Clernand's division was camped just behind Sherman, while Hurlburt's was farther back and positioned between Sherman's and Prentiss's. W.H.L. Wallace's division was farther to the rear, close to the landing.

At 4:55 A.M., Hardee's line made contact with a scouting party from Prentiss's division, three companies of the 25th Missouri Infantry. The Missouri men fired on the Confederates and began slowly falling back, fighting as they went. As they fell back, the Missouri men were reinforced by other detachments of Prentiss's division until the Confederates were facing an entire brigade. Though the Union troops were outnumbered, they fought doggedly and were able to halt the Southern advance till approximately 8:00 A.M., when they were finally overpowered and forced to withdraw toward Prentiss's camp.

When Sherman heard the first sounds of combat in front of his camp, he immediately got all his men up and under arms. Sherman directed that a battery of artillery be placed at Shiloh Church, the house of worship that would give its name to the battle. He had another battery positioned on a ridge to the south of the church. The left of Sherman's line was attacked at about the same time Prentiss's line was being pushed back into its camp. Colonel Jesse Hildebrand commanded the brigade holding Sherman's left flank. The 53rd Ohio, of his brigade, was composed of green troops who had never been under fire. The 53rd broke under the first shock of the Confederate attack and quickly ran from the field. Hildebrand's other two regiments followed the 53rd Ohio in very short order. The whole Union line was giving way. Prentiss's entire division was forced from the field, falling back to a line W.H.L. Wallace and Hurlburt were hastily forming in the rear.

McClernand brought his division forward to the support of Sherman, and fighting raged in the vicinity of Shiloh Church. The site was considered to be the key point of the battlefield because it controlled the best road from Corinth to Pittsburg Landing. Charge was met with countercharge, in some of the fiercest fighting to take place on the field that day. Sherman was supposed to be in command of all the Union troops in the vicinity, in the absence of Grant, but he was dealing with all he could handle in trying to fend off the repeated attacks in his front and flank.

Where was General Grant? He was 10 miles away in Savannah. Grant was sitting down to breakfast when he first heard the telltale boom of artillery that signaled a battle being fought around Pittsburg Landing. He sprang into action, sending orders to General Nelson to start his division at once on a march down the east bank of the Tennessee River to a point opposite Pittsburg Landing. He then boarded the steamer *Tigress* and made his way for the battlefield. When the steamer neared Crump's Landing, he had the vessel pull in close enough to shore so that he could yell out instructions to General Lew Wallace, ordering him to have his division ready to execute any orders it might receive. When the general disembarked at Pittsburg Landing, he witnessed a mob of Union refugees from the battle huddling under the brow of a hill and seeking the protection of the navy's big guns. Grant detailed two regiments to arrest the tide of stragglers and re-form them to return to the battle. He then ordered reinforcements sent to Prentiss. After making these dispositions, Grant set out in search of Sherman. He reached Sherman's line about 10:00 A.M. and found it heavily engaged. Seeing that Sherman could not hold out much longer, he sent orders to Lew Wallace to march at once to reinforce the right. Grant then rode down the line to confer with Prentiss, Hurlburt, and W.H.L. Wallace. Prentiss's men had rallied along a sunken road that ran through heavy woods. With the way the Union army had been forced back by the Confederates, this position was now the center of the Union line. It was a strong point, and Grant ordered Prentiss to hold it at all hazards.

Sherman's line was finally overpowered shortly after Grant left it, as Confederate assaults fell fast and hard along a three-and-one-half-mile front. But the battle was not going the way Johnston had envisioned it.

Grant's army was being pushed from the field, but it was being forced back on Pittsburg Landing, not toward Owl Creek. Johnston rode to the right flank of his army to personally take charge of the attack in that sector. When he arrived, he found his men bogged down and exposed to a galling fire. Johnston led a charge that broke the Union line and pushed the enemy back for three-quarters of a mile. His battle plan was back on schedule. The Federals were being driven away from the landing, not toward it. But as Johnston sat on his horse, watching the regiments that had just made the charge reform, a chance bullet from a Federal musket struck him in the leg, severing the large artery. There was no doctor nearby, and none of the staff officers present knew how to stop the bleeding, so General Johnston died from loss of blood. The death of Johnston brought about a lull in the fighting on the Confederate right that lasted for about an hour. This gave the Federals opposed to them time to regroup and reorganize.

Meanwhile, General Prentiss, with a portion of W.H.L. Wallace's command, was waging the fight of his life in the center of the Union line. Confederate attacks had forced the Union troops on either side of Prentiss's position to fall back, leaving Prentiss alone and surrounded on that part of the field. General Daniel Ruggles commanded the Confederates encircling Prentiss's men, and he launched 11 different attacks against the position. But the Union troops fought fiercely and beat back each new onslaught. Bullets were flying so thick in the air that the Confederates named Prestiss's position the "Hornet's Nest." Ruggles finally decided that if his infantry could not drive the Yankees out of their stronghold, he would blast them out with a concentrated barrage of artillery. He collected 62 cannon and unleashed an earthshaking bombardment on the Hornet's Nest. Confederate infantry advanced under cover of the big guns, and the combination was too much for Prentiss's men to withstand. They had been fighting since early morning and were almost completely exhausted. Outnumbered, outgunned, and running short on ammunition, Prentiss was finally compelled to surrender his command, approximately 2,200 men, at 5:30 P.M. The Confederates had succeeded in breaking the Union line and capturing the Hornet's Nest, but Prentiss's resolute resistance had bought precious hours of time for Grant to stabilize the situation. Nelson's division was on the way, as was Lew Wallace's division. If the remnant of his army could just hold on a little longer, these reinforcements might yet swing the tide of battle in his favor.

Grant directed that heavy siege guns be placed in a line a quarter mile inland from the landing. Smaller field artillery pieces were placed on either side of the big guns. Two gunboats, the *Tyler* and the *Lexington*, were anchored close to shore to support the land batteries. This would be the Union's last line of defense in the event the army was completely driven from the field in front. Nelson's division had arrived opposite Pittsburg Landing, and lead elements were already being ferried across. Nothing was heard from Lew Wallace, however. That officer had taken a wrong road on his march to the battlefield and had become lost. By the time the mistake was noticed and the division was countermarched back to the proper road, the greater part of the day had been wasted. Though he had been only six miles from the fighting at 10:00 A.M., Wallace's troops would not reach Pittsburg Landing till after nightfall.

General Pierre G. T. Beauregard had assumed command of the Confederate army after the death of General Johnston. Beauregard had been serving as Johnston's second-in-command and was well aware of his commander's plans and strategy. Thus far, that battle had been progressing according to plan. The Union army was giving ground all along the line, and the Confederates were driving them. After the surrender of Prentiss's command, field commanders began to reorganize their commands for a final assault on Pittsburg Landing. Beauregard sent an order to cancel the attack. His men were tired and hungry, and many of his regiments had become so intermixed during the fighting that they became an armed mob instead of a cohesive fighting force. Beauregard decided that his army had done enough for one day. They had shattered the Union army and driven it to the edge of the Tennessee River. Intelligence he had received stated that Buell's army would not reach the field in time to save Grant. The Federals would still be there in the morning, and Beauregard and his army would drive them into the river then. For now, he would allow his men to eat and rest.

Beauregard was unaware that Nelson's division was already on the scene and that more elements of Buell's army were close behind. By morning, approximately 17,000 men of the Army of the Ohio had reached the vicinity of Pittsburg Landing. Lew Wallace's division had also joined Grant's main body during the night, further strengthening his line. When dawn broke on April 7, Beauregard's exhausted Confederates would be facing about 22,000 fresh Union troops, in addition to the survivors of the previous day's battle. His failure to press his advantage in the closing daylight hours of April 6 would prove to be the turning point in the battle. The Union army had managed to survive a terrible beating, and it was now poised to deliver a little beating of its own.

When dawn broke on April 7, Grant's army was formed with Lew Wallace's division on its extreme right. Extending the line to the left were the divisions of Sherman, McClernand, and Hurlburt. Buell's army was formed to the left of Hurlburt, with the divisions of William Nelson, Thomas Crittenden, and Alexander McCook running from left to right. Grant had visited each of his division commanders in person the previous night. "I directed them to throw out heavy lines of skirmishers in the morning as soon as they could see, and push them forward until they found the enemy, following with their entire divisions in supporting distance, and to engage the enemy as soon as found." Grant was confident that the next day would end in their favor and felt that "victory was assured when Wallace arrived, even if there had been no other support." Buell's reinforcements only served to increase Grant's belief that Union forces would be triumphant.

The Union forces went forward on the morning of April 7 in search of the enemy. Beauregard had not been able to restore order to his tangled commands during the night, and many were still scattered and intermingled. Initially, the Federals met only small pockets of resistance. The majority of Beauregard's army was still lingering in the captured Federal camps, scavenging for plunder and enjoying the spoils of war. Lew Wallace's division encountered a brigade of the enemy, but it was soon overpowered and forced to retreat about a mile to the rear. Buell's troops, on the left, engaged a force of the enemy near a peach orchard. Buell's men had advanced so rapidly that they had outpaced their artillery support, and they were driven back by a fierce Confederate counterattack. When two batteries of Federal big guns arrived on the field, Buell's men took the initiative and regained the lost ground, only to be thrown back again.

By this time, the battle had become general all along the line. The fighting rivaled the combat of the previous day, as the lines surged back and forth in a constant series of charges and countercharges. There were many instances of units that had expended all of their ammunition only to continue the struggle using bayonets and clubbed muskets. General Beauregard established his headquarters near Shiloh Church. He monitored the progress of the battle to his front while he kept a watchful eye on the road to his rear. Beauregard had been promised support by General Earl Van Dorn, whose 20,000 men he believed to be in Corinth. In reality, Van Dorn's army was still in Arkansas, owing to the fact that transportation could not be obtained to ferry it across the Mississippi River. Beauregard had massed a major portion of his army in the vicinity of Shiloh Church in order to control the road he surmised Van Dorn would be using to advance to his position. When he finally realized that no reinforcements were coming, that same road became crucial as a line of retreat to Corinth. The church became the key point on the battlefield as both sides funneled more and more men into the center of their lines. Eventually, fighting on the flanks diminished while the struggle in the center continued with unabated fury.

The Confederates were mounting a strong resistance to every Federal advance, but the Federals just kept coming. Beauregard realized that without reinforcements, it was only a matter of time before his army was overpowered by the superior Union force. At 2:00 P.M., he announced his intention to break off from the battle and retire from the field. A strong rear guard, with supporting artillery, was positioned to cover the retreat of the army, and the Confederates started marching back down the road to Corinth. By 4:00 P.M., the last Confederate troops had left the field, and the Battle of Shiloh was over.

Grant made no attempt to pursue the retreating Confederates. Beauregard's army was permitted to make a leisurely march south, completely unmolested by the Federals. Grant himself stated that "an immediate pursuit must have resulted in the capture of a considerable number of prisoners and probably some guns," but no pursuit was ordered. Grant said that he "wanted to pursue, but had not the heart to order the men who had fought desperately for two days, lying in mud and rain whenever not fighting." He felt his men were "too much fatigued" to follow after the retreating enemy. The retreating Southerners had also fought for those same two days and had endured a tiresome march to reach Pittsburg Landing before the battle even started. The Confederates had received no reinforcements and did not have the luxury of being able to utilize 22,000 fresh troops, as Grant could do. The failure to pursue Beauregard was a missed opportunity to cripple or possibly destroy the Confederate army. On the morning of April 8, General Sherman led a delayed pursuit with almost two divisions of troops. As evening was beginning to fall, Sherman's force caught up with the Confederate rear guard at Fallen Timbers, only six miles from the Shiloh battlefield. The rear guard was a cavalry unit commanded by Colonel Nathan Bedford Forrest. Forrest ordered his cavalry to charge, and the Southern troopers quickly routed a regiment of Northern horsemen who were riding in advance of the main body. When Forrest tried to press his attack against Sherman's infantry, he suffered a bloody repulse. Forrest withdrew toward Corinth, and Sherman paused to bury his dead. When the interment was completed, the Federals retraced their steps back to Pittsburg Landing. The final episode of the Shiloh Campaign had taken place.

The cost of the battle was appalling to both North and South. The great battles of the Revolutionary War had witnessed nothing to compare it to. Saratoga, Cowpens, and Brandywine had produced American casualties of approximately 150, 330, and 1,300, respectively. The Battle of First Manassas, by comparison, was thought to be an epic battle of gigantic proportions, and the casualties of 4,878 in killed, wounded, and captured had been mourned by the nation as a terrible sacrifice to the horror of war. Shiloh dwarfed any battle that Americans had yet participated in. Its savagery and cost eclipsed the wildest imaginations of the people on the home front and cast a shocking numbness across the land. Some 23,746 Americans became casualties during the two days of fighting, almost 22 percent of the total number of men engaged. Larger and more costly battles were yet to be fought, but Shiloh was the first great bloodbath of the war. It swept away a national innocence that had looked upon this war as a sort of gallant adventure and replaced it with the grim horror of a struggle to the death between two courageous and determined enemies. It became a saying in the Confederacy that the South never smiled again after Shiloh.

Grant had gained his first fame at Belmont. He had become a national hero following the captures of Forts Henry and Donelson. Now his name was once more in headlines in newspapers throughout the land. The result of the battle had been a Union victory, but questions were arising about the performance of the army. How had the Confederates been able to so completely surprise the Union army? Why were there no fieldworks to protect the camps? Why was General Grant not with his army when it was attacked? As details of the fighting at Shiloh became known, many of the people who had so recently praised Grant's leadership were now calling for his removal from command. Rumors surfaced that Grant was not popular with his men. He was rarely seen by his soldiers, and when they did get a glimpse, his common dress and careworn appearance did little to inspire confidence in those he commanded. It was common to hear soldiers proclaim that John Rawlins was the brains behind Grant's success, and a popular joke in the army was that "if you hit Rawlins on the head, you'll knock out Grant's brains." A number of politicians felt that Grant had not only been responsible for the bloodbath at Shiloh; he had also lost control of his army. Alexander K. McClure, a prominent Republican and friend of Lincoln, was among this number. McClure made a trip to Washington for the sole purpose of urging Lincoln to remove Grant from command. He stated that the president listened to all his arguments, and when he had finished, Lincoln sat quietly for a few moments to reflect on his words. Then he shook his head and stated, "No, I can't do it. I can't lose this man. He fights." Lincoln decided to support this man he had never met, despite the outpouring of public sentiment against him. Grant would remain with the army. He would be given the opportunity to redeem himself the only way a soldier can: on the battlefield.

While Lincoln was deciding his fate in Washington, Grant's position with the army had been greatly altered at Pittsburg Landing. General Halleck had arrived on the scene to take personal command of the Union forces gathered there. Grant had been named second-in-command to Halleck, but the title was far from a promotion. Halleck did not know what to do with Grant, but he definitely did not want him commanding one of his armies. He sought to reprimand his subordinate for allowing himself to be surprised at Shiloh. General Buell would continue to command the Army of the Ohio, which Halleck

*Grant was a major general
during the time of the Vicksburg
Campaign. (U.S. Army
Military History Institute)*

would designate as the left wing of his combined army. The Army of
the Tennessee would serve as the right wing of that army, but Grant
would not command it. Halleck recommended George H. Thomas
be promoted to the rank of major general of volunteers and assigned
him to take over the army on April 25, 1862. According to Halleck's
reorganization, Thomas would not only be taking Grant's place in
command of the Army of the Tennessee; he would also be Grant's
superior in the coming campaign. Thomas had earned high praise
for his performance in the war to date, and his promotion to major
general was long overdue, considering the important victory he had
won at the Battle of Mill Springs several months before. His assignment to command the Army of the Tennessee was more a result of
Halleck's animosity toward Grant than an endorsement from Halleck
of Thomas's abilities, however. For his part, Thomas had played no
part in the decision to remove Grant from command. He was simply
following orders. But the embarrassment of the situation was keenly

felt by Grant and would cause strained relations between him and Thomas for the remainder of the war.

General Halleck planned a campaign against Beauregard's Confederates at Corinth, and once his army was reorganized and reinforced, he ordered it forward. The Federal army now numbered over 120,000 men, more than three times as many as Beauregard commanded. Despite this overwhelming advantage, Halleck advanced with extreme caution. He was not about to allow himself to be surprised, as Grant had done. The army would march only a short distance each day and then would stop to construct elaborate field fortifications to protect it from attack. Halleck's march was so deliberate and ponderous that the army took six weeks to cover the 20 miles between Pittsburg Landing and Corinth.

General Beauregard knew that his army could not hope to defeat the overwhelming force that Halleck commanded, and he had no intention of making a stand at Corinth. Beauregard kept his army there until the Federals arrived on the scene, then made plans to evacuate the town. As Halleck's men were engaged in digging earthworks around Corinth, preparing for a siege, the Confederates quietly slipped away, taking all of their supplies with them.

Halleck had failed to bring the enemy to battle and had allowed Beauregard to escape to fight another day. The turtle-like pace of his advance had become a source of embarrassment to the administration and a joke to the men in the army. Grant had been accused of not exercising due caution in his actions, but Halleck showed so much caution that it seemed as if he was afraid to take action at all. A change needed to be made. Halleck had shown that he was unsuited to lead an army in the field and had failed miserably in army command. The solution the administration came up with was to promote Halleck. He was called to Washington, where he was made general-in-chief of all the Union armies. This was an administrative position and would keep Halleck out of the field, but it was still a reward for the ineffective leadership he displayed while in command of the army.

In the meantime, Grant had become disheartened with the situation and had requested permission to be transferred out of Halleck's department. Halleck had been looking for a way to get rid of Grant for some time, and he quickly endorsed his request. When General Sherman learned of Grant's planned departure, he did his best to talk him out of it. Sherman argued that Grant must remain with the army and told him that the only way to restore himself to favor with the administration would be through achieving success on the battlefield. Sherman's argument convinced Grant to withdraw his request and remain with the army. Fortune smiled on him when Halleck was called east on July 10, 1862, to assume his new responsibilities, as this left Grant once more in command of the Army of the Tennessee.

Chapter 7

VICKSBURG AND THE OPENING OF THE MISSISSIPPI

The city of New Orleans was captured on April 25, 1862, the same day that Grant was replaced by Thomas as commander of the Army of the Tennessee. Combined with Grant's victories at Forts Henry and Donelson and Buell's capture of Memphis, this meant that a large portion of the Mississippi River was now in Union hands. But free navigation of the river was barred by a strong Confederate presence at Vicksburg, Mississippi. The city was positioned at a bend in the Mississippi, and Vicksburg had been turned into a formidable network of earthworks, bombproofs, and shore batteries that prevented Union shipping from passing that point and defied the Union army to try to capture the city. Lieutenant General John C. Pemberton, a native-born Pennsylvanian, commanded the Confederate army that defended the city and was charged with the crucial mission of holding Vicksburg against all odds. The possession of the city not only denied the Federals of free navigation of the Mississippi River; it also provided a vital link between the trans-Mississippi states of Texas and Arkansas and the rest of the Confederacy. If this link was broken, the South would be deprived of much-needed manpower and supplies that these states provided to the cause, and the Confederacy would be split in two. Obviously, Vicksburg was strategically important to both North and South, but Grant would have to postpone any thoughts of a campaign to capture it.

For the time being, Grant's army was fully occupied guarding all of the Southern territory acquired in the most recent campaigns. Following the capture of Corinth, the huge army Halleck had collected had been broken up and sent on different missions. General Buell's Army of the Ohio had been ordered to operate against Chattanooga in eastern Tennessee. Grant's Army of the Tennessee was ordered to hold the portions of western Tennessee and northern Mississippi that had already been captured and to send support to Buell if it should be needed. This was a difficult undertaking. Grant was forced to garrison the entire region from Columbus, Kentucky, to Corinth, Mississippi, and protect it from falling into enemy hands once more. His army was not nearly large enough to station adequate numbers of men at all of the key points he was expected to guard. Indeed, Grant believed that there was no point in making an offensive campaign against the Confederates in his department at the present time, as "the territory already occupied was as much as the force present could guard." There was little fighting done by the Army of the Tennessee during this time, except for some skirmishing with Confederate raiding parties, but Grant remembered this as the "most anxious period of the war." His army was stretched to the limit and was thinly distributed between the various posts, and if any one of them was attacked, "the best that could be done in such event would be to weaken the points not threatened in order to reinforce the one that was."

Braxton Bragg had been promoted to command the Confederate Army of Tennessee and had marched it off to the east to contest Buell's campaign against Chattanooga. There was still a sizeable force of Confederates left to face Grant, however. Major General Earl Van Dorn commanded an army in Mississippi, while Major General Sterling Price led another Confederate army in Missouri. The two generals planned a combined effort against the Federal forces in western Tennessee and northern Mississippi, and between them they could amass an army of nearly 40,000 men. In addition to this, there was a large force of Southern cavalry under the command of Nathan Bedford Forrest that was operating in Grant's rear, "making it necessary to guard every point of the railroad track back to Columbus, on the security of which we were dependent for all our supplies."

In the second week of August, orders arrived from Washington directing Grant to detach two of his divisions to reinforce Buell's army. On September 4, two more divisions were diverted from the Army of the Tennessee to the Army of the Ohio. Braxton Bragg had commenced his invasion of Kentucky, and the War Department was concentrating all available forces in the region to drive him out of the state. The buildup of Union power in Kentucky would prove successful, as Bragg was forced to retire back to Tennessee in October after losing the Battle of Perryville, but the reduction of forces in western Tennessee and northern Mississippi left Grant vulnerable to attack from the enemy.

General Sterling Price's Army of the West and General Earl Van Dorn's Army of West Tennessee had been ordered to support Bragg's invasion of Kentucky by preventing Grant from sending reinforcements to Buell. They were to keep the Union forces in their sector occupied and were instructed to join Bragg if Grant appeared to be passive and to shy away from a fight. Price and Van Dorn planned to join their forces near Iuka, Mississippi, approximately 20 miles east of Corinth. Iuka was the easternmost position held by Grant's forces in the area, and it lay astride the Memphis and Charleston Railroad, which connected it to Corinth. A supply depot was established in the town, guarded by a small detachment of troops. Grant had no intention of remaining passive in regard to the Confederate activity in his department. When it was learned that Price's army was nearing Iuka, he adopted a plan of attack suggested by General William S. Rosecrans, commander of the Army of the Mississippi. Rosecrans had previously been stationed at Iuka and was familiar with the roads and terrain. He proposed to march his army toward Iuka from the southeast and southwest, while General Edward O. C. Ord marched a division from Corinth from the northwest. The combined Union forces would surround Price's army in the vicinity of Iuka and destroy it before it could be reinforced by Van Dorn, who was approximately a four-day march away.

On September 13, Price reached Iuka, and his cavalry skirmished with elements of the Union garrison. Colonel Robert C. Murphy was in command of the town, with a force of approximately 2,000 men. Price fielded slightly over 3,000 men, and Murphy should have been able to mount a successful defense of the town until reinforcements arrived, but he ordered the place evacuated and all of the supplies to be burned on September 14. Rosecrans would order Murphy to be court-martialed for his actions in allowing Price to capture Iuka uncontested.

General Ord advanced his division along the path of the Memphis and Charleston Railroad on September 18. Rosecrans had farther to march, and the roads he was using were in deplorable condition. Additional delay was caused when one of his divisions took a wrong road and had to be countermarched back to their proper place. By the night of September 18, Rosecrans was still 20 miles away from Iuka, whereas Ord's division was within an easy march of the town. Rosecrans sent word of the situation to Grant, who was at Burnsville, about halfway between Corinth and Iuka. He informed his superior that he intended to resume his march at a very early hour on the 19th and expected to reach the town sometime that afternoon. Grant sent a copy of Rosecrans's dispatch to Ord "and ordered him to be in readiness to attack the moment he heard the sounds of guns to the south of south-east."

Rosecrans had marched to within two miles of Iuka by 4:00 P.M., when the head of his column made contact with Price's Confederates. Brigadier General Charles S. Hamilton's division was leading the column when it was suddenly attacked by Brigadier General Lewis H. Little's Confederate division. Hamilton formed a defensive line, supported by artillery and cavalry, and received the full weight of Little's attack. In the desperate fighting, the Confederates reached the spot where Hamilton's six-gun battery was posted before being thrown back. Little reformed his lines and sent the men forward again, even though he was terribly ill from malaria, which he had contracted several months earlier in Corinth. The second attack was just as fiercely contested as the first, with the Confederates reaching the Union line before being repulsed. Little ordered his men to make a third charge, and this time his troops were successful in breaking the Union position. The six guns of the 11th Ohio Battery were captured, but not before 46 of the 54 cannoneers and three of the four officers had fallen as casualties. One of the Confederates who took part in the charge remembered, "Those battery boys had so much spunk that we took on the few that were left." The 11th Ohio Battery bears the distinction of sustaining the greatest loss of any light artillery unit on either side during the war. In fact, their losses were 22 percent higher than any other battery suffered in a single engagement during the war.

The Federals had been pushed back, and it seemed as if the Confederates were on the verge of winning the battle. At this moment in time, General Little was struck in the forehead by a Federal bullet and was killed instantly. General Price ordered Brigadier General Louis Hebert to assume command of Little's division, and this change of command allowed Rosecrans time to rally his forces and bring Brigadier General David S. Stanley's division forward. By the time the Confederates resumed their attack, Stanley was in position, and the final Southern assault of the day was repulsed as darkness settled over the field. Of the slightly more than 7,600 men who had been engaged in the battle, more than 2,300 (or 30 percent) had fallen as casualties. General Price proclaimed that the fighting at Iuka was the most desperate he witnessed during the entire war.

But where were Ord and Grant while Rosecrans was fighting to prevent his army from being overwhelmed by the Confederate onslaught? A north wind had been blowing hard that day, and it caused the atmospheric condition known as an acoustic shadow, which interferes with the normal transmission of sound waves. Though Grant and Ord were just a few miles distant from the fighting, they reported that they heard no sounds coming from the direction of Rosecrans's men. Ord's orders had been to engage the enemy when he heard that Rosecrans had made contact and begun his attack, and so far as he knew, that event had not taken place. So Ord's division sat idly by, well within supporting distance of Rosecrans's hard-pressed men, oblivious to the fact that a desperate battle was being waged only a few miles away.

General Price had been in contact with General Van Dorn and had planned to rendezvous with him at Rienzi, Mississippi. On the night of September 19, he pulled his army out of Iuka and marched for a junction with Van Dorn. Rosecrans had left Price with an available escape route when he decided to march to the town using only one road, instead of the two that he had originally proposed. So the Confederates were allowed to flee the trap and fight another day. Still, Rosecrans had been successful in thwarting Price's designs at Iuka and had repulsed the Confederates with losses that were almost twice as many as were suffered by his army. He was widely lauded in the Northern press as being the hero of Iuka, and the battle was generally regarded as a Union victory. General Grant received an entirely different sort of recognition by the press. It was widely rumored that Ord's division did not fail to come to Rosecrans's aide because of an inability to hear the sounds of the battle but because Grant was drunk at the time and was unfit to command. He had been several miles away when the battle was fought, just as he had been at Shiloh, and many of the charges that followed that battle were once more revived. Grant felt that Rosecrans's action in changing his march and using only one road had enabled Price to get away, and he believed that Rosecrans was getting far too much credit for the victory, while he was receiving far too much blame for the campaign not going as planned. A rift between Grant and Rosecrans resulted, which Grant felt for the remainder of the war. In his memoirs, he dismisses the incident with the sentence, "I was disappointed at the result of the battle of Iuka—but I had so high an opinion of General Rosecrans that I found no fault at the time."

Following the Battle of Iuka, Price and Van Dorn united. Van Dorn being senior in rank, he assumed command of the combined army. Plans were made to assault Corinth for the purpose of disrupting Grant's lines of supply and communication. If the campaign was successful, Price and Van Dorn might still sweep through western Tennessee and join with Bragg, whose army was still deep in Kentucky. The Confederate army numbered approximately 22,000 men. Grant had, under his command, some 48,000 troops with which to confront Van Dorn, but they were widely separated, guarding various points in the department. Some 12,000 men were at Bolivar, just across the state line in Tennessee. Seven thousand were at Memphis, and another 6,000 were at Jackson, Tennessee. General Rosecrans was at Corinth with the remaining 23,000 men. Price met Van Dorn at Ripley, Mississippi, southwest of Corinth. From that point, the Confederates marched north until they crossed the Tennessee border. From here, a number of options were open to Van Dorn, and Grant, not knowing where the Confederates were bound for, was frozen in place and could not shift his forces until he received further indication of the enemy's intentions. By October 2, Van Dorn's movements had convinced Grant that Corinth was his objective. He sent word to Rosecrans that the Confederates were heading his way and to be prepared for an attack.

Rosecrans doubted Grant's instincts. He did not believe that Van Dorn would attack Corinth because of the extensive fortifications that had been constructed there. Instead, he believed that the Confederate objective was the Mobile and Ohio Railroad. If Van Dorn could sever that line, Rosecrans reasoned, he might be able to impede the flow of Union supplies and maneuver the Federals out of Corinth. By October 3, however, Grant's suspicions were confirmed when Van Dorn's army appeared outside the limits of the town. Rosecrans ordered troops to man the works that had been constructed by the Confederates when Beauregard was preparing to defend Corinth against Halleck in the spring. The divisions of Generals Thomas J. McKean, Charles S. Hamilton, and Thomas A. Davies were ordered to the works, north of the town, while David Stanley's division withheld to form the army reserve. Van Dorn launched his attack at around 10:00 A.M. on the morning of October 4. His plan was to assault the Union left flank and envelop the position, hoping that Rosecrans would send reinforcements from his right. Van Dorn would then make his main attack against that weakened flank and be able to force his way into the works. The plan worked but not in exactly the way in which Van Dorn had envisioned it. When the Federal left flank became hotly engaged, troops from the right were shifted to meet the Confederate threat. In the process, a large gap was opened in the center of the Union line, and by 1:30 P.M., the Confederates had found this gap and were exploiting it. The Federals broke and fell back more than a mile, to Corinth, where they took up position in a line of inner works.

At approximately 3:00 P.M., Rosecrans ordered General Hamilton to assail the advancing Confederates on their left flank. Hamilton's division had been positioned to the right of the main Federal line and was situated to deliver a knockout blow against the left and rear of Van Dorn's army. But Hamilton spent so much time preparing to make the assault that darkness began to cover the field before he could order his men forward. The fighting had concluded for the day, but both sides knew that it would be resumed on the following morning.

Van Dorn opened the action on October 4 by ordering a six-gun battery of artillery to bombard the Union position. The barrage was continued until after the sun came up, and the Federals braced themselves for the onslaught they believed would accompany the dawn. There was a lull on the battlefield, however, as the anticipated Confederate assault failed to materialize. Van Dorn had ordered General Hebert to lead an attack on the Federal right, but Hebert was seriously ill and in no condition to carry out the directive. At 7:00 A.M., Van Dorn received word of Hebert's condition, and he immediately ordered Brigadier General Martin E. Green to assume command of Hebert's troops and push the attack forward. A delay of nearly two hours ensued as Green familiarized himself with the position of the troops now under his command and made arrangements to lead the division. When he was finally ready to move, Green concentrated his attack on a Federal redoubt in his front named Battery Powell, which was held by men of Davies's division. The Confederates stormed the position and drove the Federals out, capturing all of the guns. General Hamilton's division was also stationed on the right flank, but they were able to repulse the Confederates on their portion of the line. Davies, reinforced by elements of Hamilton's command, rallied his own troops and counterattacked, driving the Confederates out of Battery Powell and recapturing the lost cannon.

General Dabney Maury threw his Confederate division at the center of the Union line after Green had occupied the Federals to his left. In some of the fiercest fighting to take place during the two-day battle, one of Maury's brigades was able to pierce the Union line and actually entered Corinth. A counterattack by a Federal reserve brigade sent them reeling back toward their own lines, however, and by 1:00 P.M., Van Dorn's assault against the town was ended. Rosecrans seemed content to simply allow the Confederates to withdraw from the field, even though he had received specific orders from Grant to pursue Van Dorn "the moment the enemy was repelled. He did not do so, and I repeated the order after the battle." Grant had dispatched Brigadier General James B. McPherson, with 4,000 troops, to reinforce Rosecrans. They were en route to Corinth and would arrive at that place by 4:00 P.M. on October 4. Grant admonished Rosecrans that if he failed to pursue the Confederates, McPherson's small force might be placed in "great peril." But Rosecrans declined to pursue the fleeing enemy. He cited the exhaustion of his men and the difficult terrain over which they must march as the primary reasons for disobeying Grant's orders and informed his commander that he would undertake the march on the following morning. Grant was disgusted by the delay and fumed, "Two or three hours of pursuit on the day of the battle, without anything except what the men carried on their persons, would have been worth more than any pursuit commenced the next day could possibly have been." Another opportunity to catch and destroy the Confederate army had been squandered, and Grant was holding Rosecrans responsible for two missed chances in as many weeks. Rosecrans would face no reprimand from his superior, however. He was being hailed in the North as the hero of Corinth, and combined with the prestige he had been accorded following Iuka, his reputation had been inflated to the point that he had been chosen by the War Department to replace General Buell in command of the Army of the Ohio.

Grant may well have felt that Rosecrans had been rewarded for a botched job at Corinth, and it is certain that he failed to obey Grant's orders regarding the pursuit of Van Dorn's force. One is left to question why Rosecrans was in command at Corinth in the first place, however. Grant had determined that Corinth was the objective of the Southern army on October 1 and had sent Rosecrans word to be ready to be attacked. Why did he not travel to the town himself and personally take charge of the efforts to defeat and destroy Van Dorn's army? As stated in his memoirs, he had already started to have misgivings about Rosecrans's leadership, stemming from his performance at Iuka. Why, therefore, did he entrust the entire battle to a subordinate in whom he had already started to lose confidence? Rosecrans's shortcomings at Corinth are a matter of record, but it would appear that Grant was also liable for a portion of the blame for not taking control of the situation and placing himself with the largest portion of his command at the point of danger.

Thus far, Grant had done little to restore his reputation with either the public or the administration. Two battles had been fought in his department since he was restored to command. They had resulted in elevating Rosecrans to army command, but for Grant, they had merely caused the allegations and criticisms he had been dealing with since Shiloh to resurface, and he began to despair of ever redeeming himself. When Grant learned that President Lincoln had given General John McClernand permission to raise an independent army to attempt the capture of Vicksburg, Mississippi, within Grant's department, it must have seemed as if his last supporter in the administration had forsaken him. John McClernand was a politically appointed officer, whose only previous military experience had been serving as a private for three months during the Black Hawk War in 1832. Lincoln had appointed him a brigadier general in May 1861 for no other reason than the fact that he was a prominent Democrat from southern Illinois. That portion of the state was strongly Democratic in their politics, and Lincoln sought to appease those citizens by naming one of their own as a general. McClernand had served several terms in Congress, and he felt that his new position in the army might serve to further his political aspirations once the war was won. With this in mind, he concocted a plan to capture Vicksburg and open navigation of the Mississippi River, which he traveled to Washington to lay before Lincoln. Federal control of the Mississippi had been a primary objective of Lincoln's since the beginning of the war. As such, he readily consented to allow McClernand to raise an independent army to accomplish the goal.

On November 9, 1862, Grant received a message from one of his subordinates informing him that rumor had it that all of the Wisconsin troops under his command were to be assigned to McClernand's army. Grant was despondent over this new turn of events and began to despair that he would ever redeem his reputation. But this despair turned to resolve as he determined to push forward with his own plans, regardless of the activities of this new rival. On that same day, Grant issued an order that was destined to increase public criticism against him and bring him to the attention of the administration in less than favorable terms. To General Stephen Hurlburt, in Memphis, he sent a telegram instructing him to "refuse all permits to come south of Jackson for the present. The Israelites especially should be kept out." Grant was attempting to halt the illegal traffic in cotton that had become so rampant within his department between Confederate brokers and Northern merchants, but his choice of words would prove to be unfortunate. Grant felt that Jews constantly disregarded his orders and were so eager to profit from the cotton trade that they were often out in front of the army instead of behind it. On November 10, he issued additional orders to Joseph D. Webster to "give orders to all the conductors [of trains] that no Jews are permitted to travel on the Rail Road southward from any point." In December, Grant lashed out by banning all Jews from his department. When news of these developments reached Washington, Lincoln and Stanton were quick to take issue with Grant's actions. The general received a reprimand and was instructed to rescind all orders he had previously issued against the Jews. It seemed as if everything he did was wrong, and the future looked dark and ominous.

Grant need not have despaired over Lincoln's backing of McClernand's plans, however. He had no way of knowing, but Lincoln had included verbiage in McClernand's orders that ensured Grant would remain master of the situation within his department. McClernand had been authorized to raise his new army with any troops that were not needed by Grant, and that would provide the loophole that would circumvent all of McClernand's designs. Of course, Grant would need all of the men McClernand raised. The general also found that he had two allies in his efforts to thwart McClernand. General Halleck and Admiral David D. Porter both opposed McClernand's fitness to command and rallied behind Grant. For his part, Grant had come to the conclusion that he could best frustrate McClernand by beating him to Vicksburg. He traveled to Cairo to meet with Admiral Porter to ask how quickly he could have his gunboats ready to cooperate in a joint expedition against the city. Porter responded that his flotilla could be ready to sail immediately.

On December 8, 1862, Grant sent a message to General Sherman instructing him to

> proceed, with as little delay as possible, to Memphis, Tennessee, taking with you one division of your present command. On your arrival at Memphis you will assume command of all the troops there, and that portion of General Curtis's forces at present east of the Mississippi River, and organize them into brigades and divisions in your own army. As soon as possible move with them down the river to the vicinity of Vicksburg, and with the cooperation of the gunboat fleet under the command of Flag-officer Porter proceed to the reduction of that place in such manner as circumstances, and your own judgment, may dictate.

Many of the troops assembled at Memphis were new regiments, raised by McClernand and sent to that place to await his arrival, at which time he would organize the army Lincoln had approved. Halleck had already given Grant permission to "take command of all the troops sent to my department and authorizing me to fight the enemy where I pleased." McClernand had raised a substantial portion of the men needed to form his army, and his arrival at Memphis to officially take command of them was anticipated daily. Grant ordered Sherman to Memphis

> to get him in command of the forces separated from my direct supervision. I feared that delay might bring McClernand, who was his senior and who had authority from the President and Secretary of War to exercise that particular command,—and independently. I doubted McClernand's fitness, and I had good reason to believe that in forestalling him I was by no means giving offense to those whose authority to command was above both him and me.

In one fell swoop, Grant had reinforced his own army and had settled the delicate question of command structure within his department. With Porter's assistance and Halleck's approval, he had incorporated McClernand's forces into his own army and was undertaking operations against Vicksburg before McClernand could arrive to contest his actions. When that officer finally reached Memphis, he would find that the new regiments he had raised were already being employed and were under the command of Sherman. Ultimately, McClernand would end up serving as a disgruntled subordinate commander in Grant's army, instead of leading the independent command he had been commissioned to raise.

Grant's intentions were to send Sherman to operate directly against Vicksburg while he sought to engage the main body of the Confederate army, under Lieutenant General John C. Pemberton, somewhere north of the city. If Pemberton's forces could be tempted to give battle north of Vicksburg, then Sherman might be able to slip in behind him and seize the city while it was lightly defended. In his memoirs, Grant clearly states this to be the objective of the operation. However, he fails to even mention how the strategy unfolded. Sherman's expedition proved to be an abject failure and ended in a bloody repulse, which is probably the reason for it being omitted from the memoirs.

On December 20, Sherman boarded his divisions on 59 transports at Memphis and began his voyage down the Mississippi River. He was accompanied by Flag Officer Porter and seven of his gunboats. The expedition stopped at Helena, Arkansas, to pick up additional troops, then made its way to Milliken's Bend, north of Vicksburg, which was reached on December 24. The fleet then sailed up the Yazoo River, losing the ironclad gunboat *Cairo* to a Confederate torpedo. The Union troops were landed at Johnson's Plantation, and Sherman began to probe the enemy forces in his front. The Confederates, under the immediate command of Brigadier General Stephen D. Lee, had constructed a defensive position in the Walnut Hills. The Chickasaw Bayou—a 50-yard-wide, chest-deep stream—fronted the Southern position and provided a natural barrier against any Federal attack. The Confederates had strengthened their position by felling trees all along their front, creating a tangled maze for any attacking enemy to traverse.

On December 26, Sherman ordered three of his brigades to perform a reconnaissance of Lee's lines, searching for a weakness. Not finding one, Sherman determined to attempt to turn the Confederate right flank. On December 28, he ordered one of his divisions forward against the Rebel right, only to be repulsed by a heavy fire from Confederate artillery. Thwarted and losing patience, Sherman decided to make a general assault, with his entire force, on the following day. He knew that the Confederate position was a strong one and estimated that his army would sustain severe casualties in capturing the enemy line, but he was quoted as saying, "We will lose 5,000 men before we take Vicksburg, and may as well lose them here as anywhere else." The Union forces numbered just under 31,000 men. Lee's forces totaled less than half that size, and Sherman was gambling that he could overwhelm the Confederate defenses by sheer weight of numbers. On the morning of December 29, he ordered his artillery to commence firing at the Southern line, in hopes of weakening them before the infantry was ordered forward. For the next four hours, the ground between the contending armies shook as the Union and Confederate big guns roared along the opposing lines. This awesome display of weaponry was probably impressive to those who observed it along the lines, but it did little damage. By 11:00 A.M., Sherman ordered the cannon fire to cease and formed his divisions for the assault. At noon, the blue wave surged forward with a cheer. The Southern defenses and the Confederate determination

proved to be too strong to be breached by the Union assault. The
Federals were thrown back all along the line, with heavy casualties.
Several more attacks were attempted, all meeting with the same result.
By the time the fighting ceased, the Federals had sustained 1,776 casualties while inflicting only 207 on the enemy. Initially, Sherman
planned to renew his attack on the following day, but by the morning
of December 30, he had been forced to admit failure and made plans to
remove his army from Chickasaw Bayou. Grant's initial foray against
Vicksburg had resulted in a lopsided defeat at the hands of an enemy
less than half his size. Events in his own department were also in a state
of chaos, as Grant himself was under attack.

On December 20, the same day that Sherman was boarding his
troops on ships at Memphis, General Earl Van Dorn appeared at Holly
Springs, Mississippi, with three brigades of Confederate cavalry. Grant
had established his main base of supplies at Holly Springs, which was
defended by Colonel R.C. Murphy and his 8th Wisconsin Infantry.
Van Dorn captured the entire garrison, along with the supplies. At the
same time, Nathan Bedford Forrest was operating in Grant's rear, destroying the railroad between Jackson, Tennessee, and Columbus,
Kentucky. Grant suddenly found himself without supplies and cut off
from communication with his superiors. It took more than a week for
him to reestablish communications and more than two weeks for food
and forage to arrive from the North. The actions of Van Dorn and
Forrest drove home to Grant the fragile nature of a line of supplies for
any army operating deep in enemy country and caused him to adopt a
course of action that would influence the future operations of Union
armies in the West for the remainder of the war.

After dispatching forces to force Van Dorn away from Holly Springs,
Grant's next priority was obtaining the necessary provisions to sustain
his army in the field. He ordered foragers to scour the countryside for
15 miles on either side of the road from Oxford to Grand Junction. Supplies were to be impressed from all citizens residing within this region.
Grant directed that these Southern noncombatants were to be left two
months' food and forage for their own use. Anything above that estimation was to be confiscated for use by the Federal army. When the
local residents protested, Grant's response "was that we had endeav-
ored to feed ourselves from our own northern resources while visiting

them; but their friends in gray had been uncivil enough to destroy what we had brought along, and it could not be expected that men, with arms in their hands, would starve in the midst of plenty. I advised them to emigrate east, or west, fifteen miles and assist in eating up what was left." The Union foragers succeeded in gathering enough supplies from the region to subsist the army for a period of two months. This lesson was not lost on Grant. When he advanced on Vicksburg again, he would do so without a strong reliance on his own line of supplies. He would look to the Southern citizens along his line of march to supply his needs, and he would live off the land.

During the first days of January, General McClernand finally made his appearance at Sherman's camp. Being senior in rank to Sherman, he assumed command of all the forces gathered there. McClernand determined to mount an offensive of his own—not against Vicksburg but against Fort Hindman, at Arkansas Post on the Arkansas River. Brigadier General Thomas J. Churchill had a garrison of some 5,000 Confederate troops at that place and had been using them to harass Union shipping on the Mississippi River. McClernand felt that this threat in the rear of the Union army must be eliminated before any further attempts were made against Vicksburg. Grant was initially opposed to the operation, calling it "an unnecessary side movement having no especial bearing upon the work before us." By January 9, McClernand had arrived at Arkansas Post with 32,000 men, as well as Porter's gunboats. For three days, the Confederate works were bombarded by the combined guns of the army and navy as McClernand prepared his army for the assault. At approximately 4:30 P.M. on January 11, McClernand was ready to launch his assault. White flags were to be seen waving from the enemy works, however, and the attack was called off. The terrible bombardment from the Union's heavy guns, combined with the overwhelming odds that they faced, convinced the defenders of the works to surrender their position. In the three days of fighting, the Union forces had sustained 1,061 casualties in killed, wounded, and missing. Confederate losses in killed and wounded totaled only about 140, but 4,791 of the fort's defenders were taken prisoner, along with 17 pieces of artillery. McClernand had been victorious in his first independent action, and the Confederate threat to the rear of the Union army operating against Vicksburg had been eliminated.

McClernand's success threatened Grant's plans for his own operations against Vicksburg. His initial thrust in the campaign had resulted in Sherman's dismal repulse at Chickasaw Bayou, while McClernand had achieved glory by his capture of Arkansas Post. McClernand would continue to exercise independent command over the forces he had with him so long as Grant remained in the rear. This circumstance seemed unbearable to Grant, and he determined to make his way to the front and assume overall command at the earliest possible moment. He stated that Sherman and Porter had both urged him to come and take charge himself and that both officers had expressed "their distrust of McClernand's ability and fitness for so important and intricate an expedition." On January 17, Grant arrived at the front and formally assumed command from McClernand. He briefly returned to Memphis to arrange the transfer of the majority of his command to the vicinity of Young's Point and Milliken's Bend, some 30 miles north of Vicksburg. General Stephen Hurlburt, along with the 16th Corps, was left in Memphis. A small garrison was also left behind at Columbus. The remainder of the department was stripped of men and guns, sent to the front to reinforce the army gathering in the Milliken's Bend area. By the end of January, approximately 45,000 men been assembled, and Grant was ready to commence offensive operations. His army was divided into three corps, commanded by Sherman, McClernand, and John B. McPherson.

How to proceed against the city and its defenders posed a real problem to the Federals, however. Natural obstacles, combined with man-made fortifications, served to make Vicksburg almost an impregnable position and severely limited Grant's campaign options. The Confederate works that lined the bluffs were far too strong to contemplate a frontal assault from the Mississippi River. The river approached south of the city before making a sharp turn to the north for approximately five miles. It then made a hairpin turn to the south, following the base of the bluffs. As such, any approaching fleet would be subjected to the plunging fire of Vicksburg's batteries for a distance of almost 12 miles. To the north of the city lay a vast region of swamps and bogs, cut by rivers and streams and overgrown with dense vegetation. Grant's engineer officer described the region as being "almost impassable in summer, and entirely so, except by boats, in winter." To make matters worse, the winter of 1862–1863 experienced heavier than average precipitation, causing water levels in the swamps and rivers to be higher than normal. West of Vicksburg, on the Louisiana side of the river, the terrain mirrored the swampy, overgrown land to the north. The ground was not suited to offensive operations and would not be until drier weather in the spring. Grant was unwilling to allow his army to pass the winter in idleness, though. Feeling that a prolonged period of inactivity would negatively affect the morale and health of his men, he determined to undertake several proposals that had little chance of success but would keep both his men and those of the enemy occupied until conditions became more suitable for campaigning.

Approaching Vicksburg from the north, by using the Yazoo River, was one of the plans adopted. Porter's gunboats inched their way along the narrow waterway, trying to reach the city by way of the back door. The vessels were constantly harassed by Confederate infantry firing upon them from either shore. When the enemy felled trees across the river, in front of and behind the ships, it looked as if Porter's fleet would be lost. The timely arrival of Sherman, with a force of Union infantry, scattered the enemy and allowed Porter to extricate his gunboats from the trap.

Another experiment tried was the digging of a canal that would cut directly across the base of the peninsula formed by the hair-pin turn of the river and allow Union vessels to sail directly to the south side of the city, without having to run the gauntlet of enemy guns posted on the bluffs. Excavating equipment was brought in, and approximately 4,000 men were put to work digging the mile-long canal. The work continued until March, when a sudden rise in the river flooded the peninsula and destroyed much of the progress that had been made. Another canal was started between Milliken's Bend and Vicksburg and was named the Duckport Canal. It was hoped that this canal would allow Union ships to leave the Mississippi River above Vicksburg and travel by means of some of the smaller rivers and bayous to a point 20 miles below the city. This project showed promise, and one small steamer actually made its way along the proposed route before the water level of the Mississippi dropped, causing the smaller tributaries to become impassable. Probing efforts were made along Steele's Bayou and Lake Providence, but all of Grant's efforts to get his army within fighting distance of Vicksburg were in vain. At least he was accomplishing his goal of keeping his

troops busy until such time as the countryside was more suitable for active campaigning. He was also keeping the enemy soldiers busy—and
a little on edge. General Pemberton may have enjoyed the luxury of
defending strong works built along natural barriers, but he still had an
immense amount of territory to defend and a limited force to defend
it with. Pemberton had to be watchful along a line that stretched approximately 200 miles. Grant's activity, and his probing expeditions,
caused Pemberton to disperse his garrison over a large area and to constantly shift troops back and forth to counter anticipated movements
by Grant. Reliable intelligence was essential for Pemberton to be able
to coordinate his activities, but he was grossly deficient in this area.
The Confederate forces at Vicksburg had no naval complement and
almost no cavalry. The lack of these branches placed Pemberton as a
severe disadvantage, and Grant must have kept him in a state of almost
constant alarm with his numerous activities and expeditions.

By the end of March, public outcry was once more directed against
Grant. Many felt that the past few months had been wasted in futile
efforts against the city, and questions about Grant's competence were
again raised. But the end of March also signaled the beginning of the
dry season around Vicksburg and witnessed the commencement of the
campaign that Grant had felt was his best opportunity to capture
the city all along. On March 29, he ordered McClernand's corps to begin
construction on a road from Milliken's Bend to below Vicksburg. This
road would cover a distance of 70 miles and would come out opposite
Grand Gulf, 25 miles south of Vicksburg. Rivers and streams needed
to be bridged, swampy areas had to be corduroyed, and trees and brush
had to be cleared away. It was difficult work, but 15,000 men accomplished it in relatively short order, and the road was completed in a
few weeks. McClernand and McPherson moved their corps down the
road, assembling around a small village appropriately named Hard
Times. Sherman's corps remained north of Vicksburg to demonstrate
against the city and keep Pemberton guessing as to what Grant's real
intentions were. Grant sought to further confuse his opponent by ordering
Colonel Benjamin Grierson, with 1,000 cavalry troopers, to make a raid
deep into enemy territory. Grierson would ride completely through the
state of Mississippi, destroying supply and communication lines along
the way and forcing Pemberton to detach large numbers of men to

defend against him. Grierson would eventually ride through to Baton Rouge, Louisiana, covering over 600 miles in just 16 days.

Having McPherson and McClernand at Hard Times was only a first step in Grant's strategy and really did little to put them closer to Vicksburg than they had been at Milliken's Bend. The Mississippi River still stood between them and the enemy, and some means must be found to get them across. On April 16, the second phase of Grant's plan was put in motion when he ordered Porter to run past Vicksburg's batteries with his gunboats. At midnight, Porter attempted to slip 12 ships past the Confederate gauntlet. Bales of hay and cotton and bags of grain were piled high on the decks to give added protection against enemy fire. The ships sailed single file as quietly as possible, hoping to pass under the guns without being noticed. Confederate pickets caught sight of the vessels, however, and prepared a warm welcome for them. Barrels of tar were set ablaze all along the shoreline on the Vicksburg side of the river. On the Louisiana bank, several houses were set on fire to add to the illumination. Porter's ships were forced to make a suicide run past the Southern big guns, with the night sky lit up as brightly as it would have been in daytime. Every one of the ships was hit repeatedly, and several were damaged to the point that they could not be controlled and drifted helplessly downstream with the current, but only one was sunk. Within a few days, the damage sustained by the ships had been repaired, and Grant was ready to transport his troops across to the enemy shore.

On April 29, Porter's gunboats bombarded the Confederate defenses at Grand Gulf preparatory to making the crossing. A six-hour barrage failed to produce any positive results, however, and Grant concluded that a landing at Grand Gulf would be too risky. The army was marched south to a point opposite Bruinsburg, and on the following day, the Union troops were safely ferried across the river. Grant was now on the Vicksburg side of the Mississippi. Grant stated that he experienced

a degree of relief scarcely ever equaled since. Vicksburg was not yet taken it is true, nor were the defenders demoralized by any of our previous moves. I was now in the enemy's country, with a vast river and the stronghold of Vicksburg between me and my base of supplies. But I was on dry ground on the same side of the

river with the enemy. All the campaigns, hardships, and expo-
sures from the month of December previous to this time that had
been made and endured, were for the accomplishment of this one
object.

Grant's landing was made unopposed. Pemberton felt that his primary duty was the defense of Vicksburg, not the defeat of the Union
army. If he marched out to fight Grant, he felt that he would be leaving the city an easy target for capture. For the time being, Pemberton
decided to watch the Federal movements and wait for an opportunity
to present itself. Grant also benefited from a faulty command structure within the Confederate army. General Joseph E. Johnston had
been sent west to assume command of that theater of operations, but
Johnston was not yet on the scene, and he and Pemberton held differing views on how the campaign should be waged. Johnston was of
the opinion that all available Confederate forces in the area should
be concentrated against Grant, setting up a decisive battle that would
expel the Federals from the region and thereby safeguard the strategic
points Pemberton was now holding. Pemberton, as already stated, felt
it his duty to cling closely to those strategic points and force the enemy
to come to him or to take advantage of any mistakes the Federals might
make. Johnston was assembling a force at Jackson, Mississippi, 45 miles
east of Vicksburg. His intention was combine this force with Pemberton's for a joint action against Grant. As of the time that the Federals
made their crossing at Bruinsburg, only 12,000 troops had been gathered at Jackson, however, and Grant was now between them and their
comrades in Vicksburg.

Grant's first goal was to capture Grand Gulf for use as a base of supplies for his army. Grant started McClernand's corps on the march toward Grand Gulf. In the meantime, Brigadier General John S. Bowen
had marched his Grand Gulf garrison several miles south, to Port Gibson.
The landscape here was rugged and thickly grown with vegetation,
making it good ground to defend against a superior foe. Bowen had
8,000 troops with him with which to oppose the 23,000 Grant had
managed to get across the river to that time. McClernand's advance
ran into Bowen's force on April 30, but only skirmishing developed.
At daylight on May 1, the Federals were ordered forward to drive the

enemy from their defensive line. Furious charges were made through-out the day, as Bowen's men were slowly and stubbornly forced to give ground and withdraw. In the end, the Confederates conducted an or-derly retreat from the field, having delayed the Union advance by a full day. Casualties amounted to about 800 on each side. Following the loss of Port Gibson, Pemberton decided not to contest the capture of Grand Gulf and ordered Bowen to withdraw his command across the Big Black River, closer to Vicksburg. Grant had his base of supplies and was strengthening his foothold on the Vicksburg side of the river.

According to Grant's initial plans for the campaign, his next objec-tive was to be the capture of Port Hudson, a Confederate stronghold downriver from Vicksburg. General Nathaniel P. Banks was to have co-operated in this venture with his army in Louisiana, but Banks notified Grant that he was not yet prepared to do so. Banks would not be ready for several weeks, and Grant was not willing to wait. He had received in-telligence informing him that General Johnston was assembling a force at Jackson and decided to attack and defeat before Johnston could join forces with Pemberton. This was a dangerous mission to undertake. To march on Jackson, Grant would have to cut himself loose from his base of supplies as he marched into the Mississippi interior. He would also be placing his army between two enemy forces. If Johnston and Pemberton were able to coordinate their actions, Grant may well find himself trapped by superior numbers, with no line of retreat and no way to subsist his army. Despite the protests of his senior officers, Grant chose to adopt this course of action, confident in his ability to defeat the Confederates at Jackson before Pemberton's army could be brought against him. The men were issued two days of rations to make the march of 45 miles to Jackson. Any additional food that was needed would be foraged from the countryside they marched through.

Pemberton aided Grant's strategy by clinging to his defensive works in Vicksburg. He believed that the further inland Grant marched, the more his army would be weakened through shortages of supplies and am-munition. Pemberton believed that if he just bided his time, the Federals would place themselves in a position where they were weak and vulner-able. Then he would attack. This allowed Grant to march on Jackson unopposed and sentenced the small Southern army there to inevitable destruction by the greatly superior Union force.

By May 12, the advance of McPherson's corps had reached Raymond, 15 miles west of Jackson. Here, the Federals ran into an enemy brigade under the command of Brigadier General John Gregg. McPherson attacked, and Gregg's outnumbered force was pushed back toward Jackson. Each side sustained about 500 casualties in the engagement. By the morning of May 14, Grant's army had reached the outskirts of Jackson. General Johnston had arrived in Jackson himself only two days before, noting that he was "too late" to be able positively impact the situation. He ordered General Gregg to take his brigade, along with that of Brigadier General William H. T. Walker, and hold the Federals long enough for him to remove the valuable stores that were stockpiled in the city. Johnston planned to retreat north, to Canton, where he would try to link up with Pemberton's army to make a stand against Grant.

The Federal attack was delayed because of heavy rain that was falling on the morning of May 14. The black powder cartridges the soldiers used in their muskets would not fire if they became wet. By 11:00 A.M., the rain slackened and the blue lines surged forward toward the city. By this time, Johnston had been able to remove most of the supplies in the town and had sent them on their way to Canton. Gregg and Walker fought a holding action until around 4:00 P.M., at which time the Federal advance took control of the city. Union casualties were approximately 300, while the Confederate defenders suffered about 800. The Federals also captured 35 cannon and all of the supplies Johnston had not been able to remove. Grant set his men to work destroying the railroad yard as he contemplated his next move. A captured dispatch from Johnston to Pemberton revealed that Johnston intended to have Pemberton join him at Canton. Grant felt that he must move against Pemberton immediately, before any such junction could be made. Pemberton had already marched out of the city with a force of 17,000 men. Pemberton's line of march was to the southeast, meaning that he was increasing the distance between himself and Johnston, instead marching toward a concentration. Grant turned his army westward, intending to give Pemberton battle while he was still widely separated from Johnston.

Pemberton had been ordered to attack Grant's army but had declined to do so, opting instead to operate against his supply line, which ran from Grand Gulf to Jackson. Early on the morning of May 16, Pemberton received another order from Johnston, directing him to march northward to join forces. Pemberton obeyed this order and faced his columns about to countermarch in the direction from which they had recently come. At about 7:00 A.M., the Confederates ran into the vanguard of the Federal army near the Champion plantation. The dominant terrain feature in the area was Champion's Hill, a crescent-shaped ridge that rose 75 feet above the surrounding landscape. Pemberton formed his line along the crest of this ridge. Pemberton had about 22,000 men with him, while Grant's army numbered 32,000. Sherman's corps had been left behind in Jackson to complete the destruction to the railroad yard and had not yet caught up with the main body. McClernand's and McPherson's corps advanced over three parallel roads, and Pemberton posted one of his three divisions to defend each of these roads.

Grant arrived on the scene at 10:00 A.M. and ordered a general attack all along his line, with McClernand on the left and McPherson on the right. The Confederates fought fiercely, but by 11:30 A.M., the Federals had pressed forward to the Rebels' main line. The opponents blazed away at one another, at close range, for over an hour. By 1:00 P.M., the Confederate line started to crack, and Major General Carter L. Stevenson's division began to retire in disorder. As men from McPherson's corps seized the crest, they also threatened to cut off the Confederates' line of retreat. Pemberton reacted to this danger by ordering General Bowen to make a counterattack with his division. Bowen's men surged forward, and a desperate struggle ensued. In some of the hardest fighting of the day, Bowen's men succeeded in driving the Federals from the crest. Grant massed his artillery to fire on the ridge, and under the cover of the big guns, the Federals seized the crest of Champion's Hill for a second time. Pemberton was unable to rally his men, and a retreat was ordered. Stevenson and Bowen withdrew their divisions from the field in the direction of Vicksburg. Major General William W. Loring found that he had been cut off from the rest of Pemberton's army. Loring was isolated and in danger of being overwhelmed. He was forced to march his division in a wide loop around the Union army to the north, where he made contact with Johnston's force. The day's fighting at Champion's Hill had been the most costly of the campaign thus far. Union losses, in killed and wounded, were more than 2,200, with total casualties of 2,457. The Confederates, being on the defensive, lost far fewer in killed and wounded, suffering about 1,400 casualties in these two categories. But 2,441 prisoners were captured by the Federals when they captured the ridge, making the total loss to Pemberton's army 3,840.

Pemberton fell back to the Big Black River, 12 miles east of Vicksburg, where his army was turned around to face the pursuing Federals. Pemberton was not yet aware that Loring had been cut off and decided to try to hold the bridge over the river until Loring's missing division could join him. He was also unaware that Grant had ordered Sherman's corps not to rejoin the main body but to march by a different route so as to place his men in the rear of Pemberton's army and cut it off from Vicksburg. Pemberton had placed Bowen's division behind earthworks on the far side of the river, supported by artillery. Stephenson's division crossed the bridge and took up positions on the opposite shore. In the early morning of May 17, Grant's pursuit caught up with the enemy at the bridge and an artillery duel ensued. While Grant was still deploying his units to assault the position, the men of Brigadier General Eugene Carr's division prematurely advanced to the attack. Carr's men went forward with a shout, completely unnerving Bowen's defenders, who were fearful of being trapped on the wrong side of the bridge with the river at their backs. Bowen's men broke and ran in wild confusion, leaving 18 pieces of artillery and 1,000 men to be captured by Carr's troops. The Confederates then destroyed the bridge, preventing any further pursuit until a new bridge could be built. The disorderly retreat of Bowen's men had cost Pemberton the loss of another 1,000 men taken as prisoners, but it possibly prevented his entire army from being captured or annihilated. If Bowen had stood fast and had fought a desperate battle to hold the bridge, the Confederates might possibly have remained at the Big Black River long enough for Sherman to have gotten in their rear. As it was, they were free to march back to their Vicksburg defenses unmolested.

Grant's army was not delayed for long by the destruction of the bridge. Union troops cut down trees and dismantled nearby buildings to furnish the wood to construct a new one. Work commenced as soon as the Confederates had departed the field and was continued into the night by the use of torches. By the following morning, the bridge was finished and Union troops were marching across. Johnston telegraphed Pemberton to evacuate Vicksburg and march his army northeast to join forces with him. Johnston felt that the city was already doomed, and he did not want to lose the army along with it. Pemberton felt that his defensive works were strong enough to repel the Federals for sufficient time to allow Johnston to raise an army suitable to lifting any siege that might result from him staying. He laid the matter before his senior commanders, and they all supported his decision to stay and defend the city. Pemberton did not know it, but by the time he got around to making the decision to stay, he no longer had much of a choice in the matter. By noon on May 18, the vanguard of Grant's army had reached the outskirts of Vicksburg, and its arrival was announced by Union cannon opening fire on the city's defenses. Like it or not, Pemberton and his army were trapped in Vicksburg.

In the space of less than a month, Grant's army had fought and won five engagements. It had inflicted heavy casualties on the enemy, captured the capital city of Mississippi, and destroyed supply and communication lines in the interior of the state. Pemberton's army had been bested on the field three times and had been forced to seek shelter behind its defensive works in the city. By the morning of May 19, Grant had his entire army in front of Vicksburg. Sherman's corps formed the right of the line, on the northern side of the city. McPherson's corps was on his left and formed the center. McClernand's corps extended McPherson's to the left and formed the southern portion of the line. The frantic retreat of Bowen's division from its position at Big Black River caused Grant to assume that the Confederates had lost their will to fight and could be easily forced out of their works. "The enemy had been much demoralized by his defeats at Champion's Hill and the Big Black," he reasoned, "and I believed he would not make much effort to hold Vicksburg." Because of this assumption, Grant ordered a general assault all along his lines.

The Union commander had been quite correct in his estimation of the demoralized condition of the Confederates at Big Black River. Their panic had been eased, however, when they marched into the strong works constructed for the city's defense. The Southern soldiers took heart when they looked out from their massive line of earthen fortifications, and their previous demoralization turned to determination.

Pemberton had been strengthening his line for seven months, and the result was truly impressive. The line began two miles above the city, at the shore of the Mississippi River. It continued, along the crest of the ridge, in an arc that ran for nine miles to a point below the city, where it connected once more to the river. Massive forts, with 20-foot-thick walls, were constructed every few hundred yards along the length of the line. These were connected by entrenched rifle pits protected by parapets. A deep ditch was dug in front of the line to impede the progress of any attacking force. Where spurs in the ridge reached out from the main line, batteries of artillery were emplaced to provide a cross fire through which an assaulting column would have to advance. The defenses boasted 128 pieces of artillery, 36 of them heavy coastal fortification guns. The ground in front of the works was filled with gullies and deep ravines, which would further hinder the plans of any attacker. All of the trees in front of the works had been chopped down to provide the defenders a clear field of fire and to deny the enemy any opportunities of concealment. All in all, there was good reason for the Confederate soldiers to take heart when they retreated into Vicksburg. The defenses they were now manning were thought by many to be impregnable, and they must have wondered if the Federals would be foolhardy enough to try to assail them.

Grant ordered an assault for 2:00 P.M. on the 19th. Sherman had been on the ground for longer than the other two corps commanders, and his men were better prepared to make the attack. His corps moved forward in good order and managed to make a lodgment at one of the Confederates' main forts before being repulsed and thrown back. McPherson and McClernand were not so successful. Their corps advanced only a few hundred yards before being forced to retire by the deadly fire directed against them. Grant's army lost 1,000 men, in killed and wounded, in this assault against the city. Confederate losses were minimal.

The attack of the 19th had proven the strength of the Vicksburg lines and had dispelled all thoughts that the Confederate soldiers in their front had become too demoralized to fight. It was evident that any future attacks against the works could result only in a costly repulse. Nonetheless, Grant determined to make another general assault along his lines. He explains his reasons for making this decision in this way:

Johnston was in my rear, only fifty miles away, with an army not much inferior in numbers to the one I had with me, and I knew he was being reinforced. There was danger of his coming to the assistance of Pemberton, and after all he might defeat my anticipations of capturing the garrison if, indeed, he did not prevent the capture of the city. The immediate capture of Vicksburg would save sending me reinforcements which were so much wanted elsewhere, and would set free the army under me to drive Johnston from the State. But the first consideration of all was—the troops believed they could carry the works in their front, and would not have worked so patiently in the trenches if they had not been allowed to try.

May 20 and 21 were spent strengthening the Union line and making arrangements for the assault. The attack commenced at 10:00 on the morning of May 22, with every cannon in the Union army bombarding the Confederate positions. The three corps moved forward amid a shower of shot, shell, and small arms fire. All three corps were able to claim lodgments being made in the enemy line, but nowhere could it be broken. In many cases, Federal troops advanced to the very parapets of the Confederate works only to be trapped there, unable to move forward or back, pinned down by the murderous fire coming from their front. McClernand reported that he had captured several enemy entrenchments in his front and requested reinforcements in order to exploit his gains. Grant complied by sending him another division and ordered Sherman and McPherson to renew their attacks to provide a diversion in favor of McClernand. The blue lines surged forward again, only to meet with the same result as the first attack. Grant stated, "This last attack only served to increase our casualties without giving any benefit whatever." Union losses topped 3,000 men in this attack, while the Confederate defenders lost fewer than 500. Southern troops felt that they were avenging their losses at Champion's Hill and Big Black River and were confident that they could destroy the Union army if it would continue to make such futile attacks.

But Grant was now convinced that he could not take Vicksburg by storm. He would order no more frontal assaults to be made against the city's defenses. Instead, he settled down to begin siege operations

against the defenders and the citizens of Vicksburg. A series of approaches were begun—deep trenches that were dug in the direction
of the enemy works. The army's artillery, as well as the big guns of
Porter's naval vessels, began a round-the-clock bombardment of the
city that was to continue for the next six weeks. Pemberton, having
a limited supply of ammunition and little hope of receiving more, ordered his gunners to respond to the barrage only when it was abso-
lutely necessary or when it appeared as if the enemy was about to make
a rush upon his works. Pemberton's lack of artillery ammunition made
it possible for the Federal soldiers to dig their approaches in relative
safety, so long as they did not expose themselves to small arms infantry fire. Day by day, the work progressed as the Union army inched its
way forward toward the Confederate line. Conditions within the city
deteriorated on a daily basis as well. Pemberton did not have enough
troops to form a reserve, and therefore he could not rotate men off
the line for a rest period. All of his available soldiers were committed
to enduring the fearful bombardment right where they were, in trenches
on the front line. This constant exposure to battle conditions began
to wear on the defenders both physically and mentally. To add to
their discomfort, food supplies in Vicksburg began to run low. Soldiers and citizens alike suffered from the lack of food. As the situation
became more desperate, mules were slaughtered for their meat, and
many people were reported to have caught and eaten rats within the
city. Wallpaper was even stripped from houses and businesses so that
the glue used to affix it could be eaten. Medical supplies were also in
short supply and were quickly used up by the ever-mounting casualties caused by the siege. The suffering of the soldiers and civilians was
extreme, but the resolve to hold their city remained resolute. Many
citizens vacated their houses and occupied local caves to escape the
constant bombardment, but they gave no thought to quitting the city
or surrendering their cause.

Pemberton's main goal in defending Vicksburg was to give Johnston
time to raise an army sufficient in size to attack Grant and raise the
siege. The Vicksburg defenders were buying this precious time with
their lives, but regrettably, the Confederacy did not possess the resources to allow Johnston to accomplish this feat. General Robert E.
Lee had begun his Gettysburg Campaign in the East, and no troops

*Grant appeared here in the fall
of 1863, following the capture of
Vicksburg. (U.S. Army Military
History Institute)*

could be shifted from that theater of operations. General Braxton
Bragg's army, in Tennessee, was facing an aggressive opponent in the
person of General William S. Rosecrans. If Bragg's army was weakened to reinforce Johnston, Rosecrans would be free to drive Bragg
completely out of Tennessee, and that state would be lost to the Confederacy. Johnston had been able to increase the size of his army to
about 30,000 men, through the addition of many raw recruits, but
many of them were without arms or ammunition, and the army lacked
the wagons to transport the supplies it did have. Grant, in contrast,
was being constantly reinforced by way of Memphis. Fresh troops and
piles of supplies and ammunition were regularly coming into his lines.
The size of his army had been increased to the point that he had sufficient men to conduct his operations against Vicksburg, while at the
same time he was constructing a line to his rear, facing in the direction of Johnston's army, to prevent any interference to his plans from
that sector. Vicksburg was being shelled and starved into submission,
and there was virtually nothing Johnston could do to prevent it. On

June 15, he notified the government in Richmond, "I consider saving Vicksburg hopeless."

Pemberton and his army would hold on for almost three more weeks. By July 1, the garrison had lost about 10,000 men to wounds and sickness, leaving the troops on the front line spread dangerously thin. Pemberton feared that if Grant launched another general assault, he might not have sufficient troops to repel it. Feeling that the city was doomed, Pemberton asked his senior officers if they felt that the garrison could fight its way out of Vicksburg and march to a junction with Johnston. All of his commanders responded that their men were too weak and physically distressed to attempt such a move. This left Pemberton to choose between holding his position and selling the lives of his men in a desperate last stand or meeting with Grant to seek honorable terms of surrender. Not wanting to increase the useless expenditure of lives in forestalling a foregone conclusion, Pemberton chose the latter course. On July 3, Pemberton ordered that white flags of truce be raised along the center of his line. "Hostilities along that portion of the line ceased at once. Soon two persons were seen coming towards our lines bearing a white flag. They proved to be General Bowen, a division commander, and Colonel [L. M.] Montgomery, aide-de-camp to Pemberton." The emissaries carried a message from Pemberton asking for an armistice, during which time surrender terms could be discussed. Grant agreed to the armistice and ordered all of his men to cease firing. He sent word to Bowen and Montgomery that he would meet with Pemberton, between the lines in front of McPherson's corps, at 3:00 P.M. At the appointed hour, Pemberton appeared in front of his lines, accompanied by Bowen and Montgomery. Grant, along with McPherson and several other officers, advanced to meet him. The parties came together beneath a stunted oak tree between the lines. Grant was well acquainted with Pemberton, and the two had served together in the Mexican War. He greeted Pemberton amiably, but that spirit of friendship was soon to dissolve. Grant demanded the unconditional surrender of Pemberton's army. This the Confederate commander was unwilling to accept. He offered to surrender the city to the Federals, so long as they permitted him to march his army away with all their arms and artillery. Grant flatly declined to accept such a proposal. Pemberton snapped, "The conference might as well end," and negotiations between Grant and Pemberton ceased temporarily. Grant had agreed to send a formal letter detailing his terms of surrender by 10:00 that night, however. Grant's written terms allowed that all of Pemberton's men would be paroled once the garrison surrendered. They could then return home and await their official exchange before being permitted to once more serve in the military. But the Confederate army must be surrendered. There would be no marching away, no joining with Johnston's forces. The defenders must lay down their arms and submit to their fate as prisoners. Pemberton did not like the terms, but he had little room to negotiate. He knew that his army could not resist another general assault on his line and anticipated that the Federals would be making such an effort shortly. He did not know that Grant had already ordered an attack to be made on July 6. With no good options available to him, Pemberton accepted Grant's terms. The Confederate army, numbering slightly less than 30,000 men, was officially surrendered on the fourth of July, and Vicksburg was fairly won. The Mississippi River was now in Union hands above and below Port Hudson, and the Confederacy was effectively split in two. Grant had won the crowning victory of his military career thus far, and he recognized the significance of his accomplishment. Combined with the decisive Union victory at Gettysburg, which had taken place the preceding day, the fall of Vicksburg marked a turning point in the war. Grant noted that these two momentous events "lifted a great load of anxiety from the minds of the President, his Cabinet and the loyal people all over the North. The fate of the Confederacy was sealed when Vicksburg fell. Much hard fighting was to be done and many precious lives were to be sacrificed; but the morale was with the supporters of the Union ever after."

Chapter 8

CALLED TO CHATTANOOGA

The capture of Vicksburg caused Grant to resume his place among the great Union leaders of the war. Public outcry and denunciation now turned to adoration for the conquering hero. Union spirits soared because of his victory in Mississippi and that of General George G. Meade at Gettysburg. General William S. Rosecrans had begun his Tullahoma Campaign in Tennessee and was driving Braxton Bragg's Confederate army through the length of the state. The capture of Chattanooga seemed inevitable, and its fall would open the heartland of the South to invasion and spell the beginning of the end for the Confederacy. For two long years, the efforts of the Northern armies had been subjected to failure after failure. Many supporters of the Union had despaired of ever being able to defeat the Confederates and force the Southern states back into the fold. Now, it looked as if the end was in sight. The Union armies were making progress, and Southern forces had been thrown on the defensive in every theater of operations. A little more time and a little more perseverance might see the issue through to its successful conclusion.

President Lincoln sent Grant a personal letter of thanks following the capture of Vicksburg. He also sent him word of his promotion to the rank of major general in the regular army. Grant was already a major general, but the rank was in the volunteer service only. It was a temporary grade that would only be in effect as long as the war continued. His new promotion ensured that the rank he held would be permanent.

After spending a short time in Vicksburg, Grant took a trip to New Orleans. It was a long-deserved vacation from the stress and responsibilities of command. He was well known to many of the Union officers stationed in the city and found himself something of a celebrity, as he was wined and dined and treated like the guest of honor wherever he went. There had not been much talk of his drinking during the Vicksburg Campaign, but it was reported that he imbibed freely during his New Orleans excursion. He attended a review that was held in his honor and, upon returning to his hotel, was injured when his horse inexplicably bolted and fell, trapping the general's leg under the animal's weight. Grant had to be carried to his hotel room on a litter and was forced to spend the next two weeks in bed. When he finally was well enough to return to Vicksburg, his wife and four children were waiting for him. He took up residence in a house in the city, and the family spent a few happy months together.

In the meantime, the campaign in Tennessee had become quite active. Bragg's Confederate army had been maneuvered across the entire length of the state. General Rosecrans's Union army stood at the very gates of Chattanooga, and the country braced itself for news of the expected bloodbath that would result when he attacked the fortified city. No such news was forthcoming. Rosecrans was able to win a bloodless victory by maneuvering the Confederates out of Chattanooga. Bragg's army was forced to quit the state and withdraw into northwest Georgia. Rosecrans pursued, but his forces were widely separated. Bragg looked for an opportunity to pounce on a portion of the Union army and destroy it before support could arrive. The Confederates were operating from a position of strength now. For one of the few times in the war, they would actually outnumber their opponents on the battlefield. The reason for this was that the Confederate high command was able to do for Bragg what it had not been able to do for Pemberton. Lieutenant General James P. Longstreet's corps had been detached from the Army of Northern Virginia and sent to assist Bragg. With these reinforcements, Bragg felt certain he could defeat Rosecrans and recapture much of the territory that had been lost in the campaign.

Bragg fell on Rosecrans's army on September 19, at Chickamauga, Georgia. For the next two days, one of the bloodiest battles of the war was fought. On the second day, the Confederates broke the Union line, and a large portion of Rosecrans's army, including the general himself, fled from the field for the defenses of Chattanooga. General George H. Thomas assumed command of the portion of the army that remained. Thomas stood his ground and repulsed all of the attacks made against his position, saving the army from being routed and earning for himself the nickname "Rock of Chickamauga." When night fell, he too retired to Chattanooga.

Bragg's army advanced and took up strong positions on the hills that ringed the city. Batteries were emplaced to prevent Union ships from reaching Chattanooga by means of the Tennessee River. Rosecrans's army was trapped. It was Vicksburg in reverse. Bragg intended to starve the Union army into submission, to see how well they liked eating mule meat. The only means of supply for the defenders of the city was a tortuous mountain road that came from Bridgeport, Alabama. The road was so treacherous that only small loads could be packed on the mules making the trip, and most of the forage had to be fed to the animals that were carrying it, leaving precious little when they reached their destination. It was estimated that as many as 10,000 horses and mules died while bringing supplies to Chattanooga, and their carcasses littered the route. The situation in the Union army deteriorated rapidly, and food became so short that guards had to be placed at the horse troughs when they were fed to prevent the men from stealing the forage. The defeat at Chickamauga seemed to have unnerved Rosecrans, and for the first few weeks after the battle he acted like a man who did not know what to do. The administration in Washington feared that the army would be lost if drastic measures were not taken immediately. The elimination of Rosecrans's army and the restoration of Confederate control over the state of Tennessee would almost undo all of the positive gains that had been made that year and would place the Union no closer to winning the war than it had been at the close of 1862.

The capture of Vicksburg had earned Grant a reputation as a general who got things done, regardless of circumstances. At the present, his

army was not employed. Units sent to reinforce him during the Vicks-
burg Campaign had already been ordered to other theaters, where their
services were more sorely needed. Now, the administration decided that
Grant could best serve the cause in another location. On October 10,
1863, he received orders from the president to travel to Indianapolis,
Indiana, to meet with Secretary Stanton and receive his instructions.
Grant and the war secretary had never before met in person. Though
Grant's name had become famous, his face was not yet so well known.
When Grant and his party got off of the train, Stanton came over to
greet them. He passed right by the plain, common-looking man he had
come to meet and grasped the hand of one of the officers on Grant's
staff. "How are you General Grant?" Stanton asked. "I knew you at
sight from your pictures."

Stanton informed Grant that the administration wanted him to
go to Chattanooga and take charge of the situation there personally.
Lincoln and Stanton made sure that he was given the authority necessary to make any decisions he felt justified in lifting the siege and
saving the garrison by giving him command of all Union forces west
of the Allegheny Mountains, with the exception of those in Louisiana.
Command of the Army of the Tennessee was turned over to Sherman,
and Grant made plans to travel to Chattanooga.

The general was still suffering the effects of his accident in New Orleans, and the arduous trek across the mountain road from Bridgeport
was physically taxing to him. He arrived in the city late on the night
of October 23 in a pouring rain. He was in so much discomfort that he
had to be lifted from his horse by members of his staff. His first order
of business was to meet with General Thomas. Rosecrans had been
relieved of command, and Thomas had been assigned to take his place.
Thomas sent members of his staff scurrying to announce Grant's arrival
to the leading generals of the Army of the Cumberland and to bring
them to headquarters to meet with their new commander. Thomas was
so involved in arranging this meeting that he failed to notice Grant's
clothing was so drenched that he was creating puddles of water where
he sat. When one of Grant's aides called attention to the commander's
condition, Thomas "begged his newly arrived chief to step into a bedroom and change his clothes. His urgings, however, were in vain. The

general thanked him politely, but positively declined to make any additions to his personal comfort, except to light a fresh cigar."

When Thomas's subordinate commanders arrived, the first order of business was discussing how they could raise the Confederate siege and eliminate the supply problem to the city. Grant was informed that plans were already being put in motion to create a new supply line, the "cracker line" as it was being called. Rosecrans's top engineering officer, Brigadier General William F. Smith, had come up with the idea, and Rosecrans and Thomas had endorsed it. In fact, Rosecrans was just about to begin the operation when he received notification that he was being relieved. Grant was briefed on the details. He listened attentively and announced that he would ride out the following day to examine if the plan was feasible or not.

Smith's plan called for a movement to be made against a Confederate position opposite Brown's Ferry on Moccasin Point, just below Chattanooga. The Lookout River flowed between the Federals and the enemy on the opposite shore. A narrow valley ran through a series of sharp hills, which provided an open supply route to Bridgeport. The terrain on the Confederate side was extremely rugged and easily defended. As such, there was a relatively small number of Southern troops assigned to guard it. Thomas maintained that if it could be wrested away from the enemy, he would be able to hold it against anything the enemy might throw at him. The plan called for sending an expeditionary force down the river, at night, to land stealthily on the Confederate side. If the defenders could be taken by surprise, the position might be captured before General Bragg knew what was happening. Grant gave his approval after visiting the ground, and the operation was slated to take place on the night of October 26.

After dark on the 26th, Brigadier General William P. Hazen readied 1,800 men to make the hazardous trip down the river, nine miles away from Brown's Ferry. By 3:00 the following morning, they were all embarked on 60 pontoon boats and were floating with the current. If the little flotilla was spotted by the enemy, it was hoped that the sheer distance they were traveling would confuse the Confederates by not giving them any definite idea of where the troops were destined for. This should prevent the Confederates from being able to concentrate their forces to oppose the landing. General William F. Smith had another 2,200 men at Brown's Ferry, just out of sight from the Southerners across the river. If the landing was successful, Smith was to cross his men to cooperate with Hazen.

Hazen's men made the journey without being detected and landed on the Confederate side unopposed. They quickly overpowered the enemy posted there and by 5:00 A.M. were in control of all the hills covering the ferry. Smith set to work constructing a pontoon bridge across the river, and by 10:00 A.M., it was completed and his troops were marching across, bringing much-needed artillery with them. The valley pass was in Union hands, and the entire operation had been conducted without one Federal soldier being killed. Thomas's men were firmly embedded in the mountainous country, and Bragg would have to make a concentrated effort with a large portion of his army to dislodge them. The siege was lifted, and a secure supply line to Bridgeport had been opened. Food and munitions could start rolling in to the needy troops in Chattanooga. Grant had been the victim of bad luck numerous times throughout his life. At Chattanooga, his luck changed. Though the plan to open the cracker line was not his, and though he had virtually nothing to do with it beyond approving an operation that was already in motion, he received all the credit for lifting the siege. Newspapers reporters assumed it had all been his brainchild and sang the praises of the man who had captured Vicksburg and had now prevented Chattanooga from suffering the same fate. Although Grant had nothing to do with the erroneous information being spread, he also took no steps to correct it or assign credit for the operation to those to whom it was due. In his memoirs, Grant stated that General Smith had been "instrumental in preparing for the move which I was now about to make." The fact is that Smith had been entirely responsible for planning the operation. Grant had merely rubber-stamped his approval to a maneuver that would have been undertaken whether or not he had been assigned to Chattanooga. Had Rosecrans been retained in command for a few more days, he would have restored his reputation and earned the thanks of the nation. As it was, Grant ended up being in the right place at the right time, and the laurels of victory fell to him.

Grant was not the only Federal soldier being sent to Chattanooga. The administration had forwarded all available units to the aide of the trapped garrison. The 11th and 12th Corps had been detached from the Army of the Potomac and had been sent south, under the command of Major General Joseph Hooker. Sherman's Army of the Tennessee was coming from Vicksburg, looking forward to a reunion with their former commander. Hooker's Eastern veterans had been on the scene since before the cracker line was successfully opened. Thomas had ordered Hooker to halt his men at Bridgeport, however, reasoning that having them in the city would be of no benefit to the Union cause until provisions could be made to feed them once they arrived. Sherman's men would reach Chattanooga soon, and the time was now right to effect a concentration of all Union forces.

Now that a supply line had been opened, Grant was anxious to take the initiative and begin offensive operations against Bragg's Confederate army. Washington was worried over the safety of General Ambrose Burnside's army at Knoxville, however. The administration feared that the opening of the cracker line would induce Bragg to shift his attention toward Burnside, whose 12,000-man army would now prove an easier target than the defenders of Chattanooga. General James P. Longstreet's corps had already been shifted north to besiege Knoxville, and Burnside was facing a superior force of some 20,000 men. Grant was ordered to make a diversion that would assist Burnside by forcing Bragg hold his position instead of reinforcing the effort against Knoxville. Washington directed that an attack be made on Missionary Ridge and set the date for November 7. Grant ordered General Thomas that he would be making the assault with his Army of the Cumberland, and Thomas was horror-struck. He argued that the Army of the Cumberland was still in too much of a weakened condition to undertake such a mission. He also advised that the Confederate position was too strong to be taken by storm at this time and cautioned that the city would be left open to capture by the enemy if the effort failed. Thomas suggested the operation be postponed until Sherman's army had arrived. After personal reconnaissance and due deliberation, Grant agreed with Thomas's recommendations and countermanded the order to attack. Burnside would have to fend for himself for now.

General Sherman reached Chattanooga on November 14, in advance of his army, which had just marched into Bridgeport. Grant, Sherman, and Thomas conducted a tour of the army's positions and developed a plan of attack. Sherman was to form his army to the left of Thomas's, where he would be in position to launch an attack against the Confederate right flank on Missionary Ridge. The date for the commencement of the operation was set for November 21. Sherman returned to Bridgeport to hasten his army forward, but heavy rains slowed its progress. Bragg's men compounded the situation by sending rafts down the river to break up the pontoon bridges. The Army of the Tennessee missed its target date and had still not reached Chattanooga by November 22. General Thomas suggested that further delay might be avoided if the advance of Sherman's army joined with Hooker's 11th Corps to make the attack on Missionary Ridge. The remainder of the Army of the Tennessee could then cooperate with Hooker's 12th Corps in making the demonstration against Lookout Mountain. Grant approved the plan and decided to put it into operation on November 23, but Sherman could not meet this deadline, as his troops were not yet up and in position.

On November 23, Grant ordered Thomas to make a reconnaissance in force against Orchard Knob, a small hill in front of Mission-

A view of Missionary Ridge, at Chattanooga, looks from the Union position at Orchard Knob. Troops from the Army of the Cumberland stormed up these heights to break the Confederate line and end the siege of the city. (U.S. Army Military History Institute)

ary Ridge. Supported by artillery, Thomas's Army of the Cumberland surged forward and was able to drive the enemy from the knoll. The following day, General Hooker was directed to assault the Confederate left by making a charge against Lookout Mountain. Hooker's troops advanced up the steep slopes of the mountain, where they were engaged by the Southern defenders. A heavy fog enveloped the slopes and obscured the view of spectators in Chattanooga and on Missionary Ridge. The progress of the fighting and the positions of the opposing lines could only be tracked by the sound of the artillery and small arms fire, prompting the fight to be named the Battle above the Clouds. Hooker's men pressed forward, but after three hours of hard fighting, they had only pushed the enemy back about 400 yards. When darkness brought about a close to battle, the fog lifted, and the campfires of the opposing troops could be seen lining the mountain from its base to its summit. During the night, the Confederates withdrew, however, and by morning a U.S. flag could be seen fluttering from the crest.

Sherman was now in position, and Grant ordered his main attack to be made on November 24. Hooker's troops were instructed to locate and attack the Confederate left flank. General Thomas had urged that the main Union assault be made there, but Grant intended for Hooker's attack to be made only as a diversion. His main effort was to be made against the Confederate right, at Tunnel Hill, by Sherman's army. Thomas's Army of the Cumberland was to hold its position in the center and await developments. If either flank was turned, Thomas would then be unleashed against the center of the Rebel line.

Sherman's attack commenced at approximately 10:00 A.M. on November 25. Six divisions were sent forward in crashing waves against the Confederate defenses, but each attack was repulsed with bloody losses by the outnumbered defenders. By that afternoon, Sherman had failed to dislodge the enemy, though his forces had suffered some 2,000 casualties. Hooker was having better success on the Confederate left. By 3:00 P.M., he had located the enemy flank and was driving it back, planting his banners on the crest of the mountain ridge in his sector. Grant observed Hooker's progress and now ordered Thomas to make a limited assault in his front, in hopes that it would enable Sherman finally take Tunnel Hill. Thomas was instructed to advance his army only to the base of Missionary Ridge and capture the rifle pits located

*Grant examines the rugged
terrain at Lookout Mountain
following the famous Battle
above the Clouds. (U.S. Army
Military History Institute)*

there. General Gordon Granger was assigned to lead the charge of
Thomas's men, and 20,000 troops would be committed to the effort. The
men of the Army of the Cumberland were eager to avenge the loss
at Chickamauga and redeem their loss of reputation resulting in their
being trapped and besieged in Chattanooga. They moved forward, determined to accomplish their mission and prove their worth as soldiers.
They advanced steadily through the hail of artillery and musket fire
directed against them until they had reached the base of the mountain.
After a short struggle, the Confederates occupying this advanced line
retreated and scampered up the slope.

Thomas's men had gained their objective but in doing so had
placed themselves in great danger. Bragg had constructed defensive
lines along the entire face of the mountain. The Federals had captured
the line constructed along the base, but they were now subjected to a
plunging fire from the other lines above. The victory of Thomas's men
had resulted in them being trapped in an untenable position. Casual-

ties were mounting from the deadly fire being rained down on them from above. It was clear that they could not remain where they were without seeing their ranks decimated. To retire from the rifle pits would be almost equally costly, as they would have to withdraw over open ground and would sustain heavy casualties in returning to their starting point while failing to accomplish their mission. To advance up the slope against a firmly entrenched enemy seemed like suicide. Grant and Thomas watched, trying to decide what to do next, when fate stepped in and decided the issue for them.

The men of the Army of the Cumberland were seasoned veterans who had served on many hard-fought fields and were well acquainted with warfare. They were aware of their predicament and of the options available to them. As a group, they seem to have collectively determined that if they were to die, it was better to do so going forward than to be shot down remaining where they were or retreating to the rear. As Grant and Thomas looked on, men could be seen making their way up the slope. At first, it was just individuals and small groups, but soon all 20,000 were ascending the mountain with a yell. Grant could not believe what he was seeing. He felt that the impetuous charge would surely meet with disaster and turned to Thomas to ask, "Who ordered those men up the ridge?" Thomas responded that no order to advance had been given. Grant then turned to Granger to ask if he had issued such orders. "No," Granger replied, "they started without orders. When those fellows get started, all hell can't stop them." Grant watched helplessly, unable to control or influence the events that were unfolding before him. He was heard to mutter, "It's all right if it turns out all right. If not, someone will suffer."

The Union assault swept steadily forward. The Army of the Cumberland men were not to be denied. So reckless and fearless was their charge that it led to speculation that the troops making it were drunk. But it was determination, not liquor, that sustained the men. Walking where they could and climbing on their hands and knees when they couldn't, the Federals drove the enemy before them as they ascended the slope. The scene was one of chaos, especially in the Confederate ranks. Unnerved by the unexpected move and demoralized by the wave of retreating comrades escaping their Union pursuers, the other defensive lines began to crack. The Confederates along the summit emulated the Union advance when the blue-clad lines approached their po-sition. At first, the Southerners began to retreat singly and in small groups, throwing down their weapons and fleeing for the rear. Soon, the entire line caved in and melted away. As General Bragg looked on, he stated, "A panic, which I had never before witnessed, seemed to have seized upon the officers and men, and each seemed to be struggling for his personal safety, regardless of his duty or his character."

Union banners now fluttered from the crest of Missionary Ridge. The Confederate army had been pried from its stronghold and was now in full retreat. A glorious victory had been won, but Grant did not seem to be elated over the success. When one of his officers congratu-lated Grant for the victory, he gruffly snapped, "Damn the battle! I had nothing to do with it." To be sure, his influence on the outcome of the campaign had been minimal and could even have proved det-rimental had it not been for the fortunate twist of fate caused by the impetuous charge of the Army of the Cumberland. He had nothing to do with the planning of the cracker line that had lifted the siege. His main attack, against Tunnel Hill, had proven to be a dismal and costly failure. The demonstration against the Confederate left had shown that Thomas had been correct in advising that the main Federal effort be made there. All in all, the siege of Chattanooga would have prob-ably been lifted and Bragg's army would probably have been defeated even if Grant had never been sent to the city. But he was sent, and he was in command of all Federal forces operating in and around Chat-tanooga. As such, he was in line to receive full credit for the victory. Grant accepted full credit as well. He failed to acknowledge that others had been largely responsible for the success that had been achieved. In his memoirs, he goes so far as to state that the impetuous charge up Missionary Ridge had been made under his orders. "Without awaiting further orders or stopping to reform, on our troops went to the second line of works; over that and on for the crest—thus effectively carry-ing out my orders of the 18th for the battle and of the 24th for this charge." Grant had personally countermanded the attack orders for the 18th and had given explicit instructions that the attack on Missionary Ridge was to stop at the rifle pits. When the Army of the Cumberland exceeded these orders, he became agitated and angry and demanded to know by whose authority the charge was being made, asserting that someone would pay if it failed. Halleck had been promoted following Shiloh, and Rosecrans had been elevated to army command after Iuka and Corinth. Grant was not going to allow any rivals to benefit from the victory at Chattanooga, so he surreptitiously accepted all glory for the campaign himself.

And glory followed the success at Chattanooga like an avalanche. Combined with his capture of Vicksburg, this latest victory propelled Grant to a level of national prominence he had never before dreamed of. His virtues and leadership qualities were extolled in the press. He was wildly popular among the rank and file of the Western army, as the men believed that he had been responsible for their recent string of successes. His name became a household word, and every schoolboy in the North adopted him as one of their heroes. So great was his fame that it was even discussed in political circles that he might be a worthy candidate to assume the mantle of the Republican Party and deny Lincoln a second term in the 1864 election. Grant's fame and popularity became so great that it worried President Lincoln. Lincoln wanted a second term in office, but he feared the Grant mania that had seized the nation might unseat him. He secured an interview with a man from Galena who was a friend to both himself and Grant and inquired about the general's future intentions. Lincoln was told that Grant had no interest in becoming president. He did not desire to have anything to do with politics. When newspaper reporters pressed Grant for insight into his future intentions, he told them that he could only do one thing at a time, and for the present, he had his hands full prosecuting the war to its final conclusion. So far as politics was concerned, he said that his only aspirations were to become mayor of Galena just long enough to see that a descent sidewalk was built to the railroad station.

Back in Washington, a great deal of conversation was taking place regarding the Army of the Potomac. Major General George G. Meade had come under severe criticism for allowing Robert E. Lee's Army of Northern Virginia to escape following the Union victory at Gettysburg the previous July. Most of the criticism was unfounded, but Meade had lost favor with the administration, and there was serious talk about replacing him. General George H. Thomas seemed to be the officer most of the politicians preferred as a replacement. In the meantime, Congressman Elihu Washburne introduced a bill in the House

of Representatives to revive the rank of lieutenant general in the U.S.
Army. George Washington was the only officer in American military
history to hold this distinction, and following his retirement it had
been decided to retire the rank as well. No other officer was to be rated
the same as Washington. To be sure, General Winfield Scott had been
promoted to lieutenant general, but it was only a brevet, or temporary,
grade. Reinstating the grade of lieutenant general as a permanent rank
would require a vote of Congress. Washburne was from Grant's hometown, and everyone knew that if the bill passed, Grant would be named
to the rank and would be in command of all the Union armies. Few opposed Grant's assignment to overall command, but there was considerable argument over whether he should be raised to so lofty a plateau as
Washington now enjoyed by granting him the coveted rank. After considerable debate, the bill was found to have enough votes to pass. On
March 4, 1864, Grant wrote to Sherman surmising that he was about
to be confirmed as the first lieutenant general since Washington. "The
bill reviving the grade of lieutenant-general in the army had become
law, and my name has been sent to the Senate. . . . I now receive orders
(March 3) to report to Washington immediately in person, which indi-
cates either a confirmation or a likelihood of confirmation." Assigning
Sherman to command of the combined armies in and around Chattanooga during his absence, Grant made his way to Washington to meet
with President Lincoln. The general who had made his reputation in
the West was now going east to see if he could achieve the same results
against Robert E. Lee and the famed Army of Northern Virginia. With
Grant poised to take over direction of the entire Union army, even talk
of replacing Meade ceased in the halls of Congress.

Chapter 9

GENERAL-IN-CHIEF

Grant arrived in Washington on March 8, accompanied by his oldest son and several members of his staff. He took a room at Willard's Hotel, and the front desk clerk was astonished when he turned the guest register around to read the name that had been inscribed. The man before him hardly matched the image he had in his mind of what the famed General Ulysses S. Grant would look like. A guest at the hotel recorded the following description:

> A short, round-shouldered man, in a very tarnished major-general's uniform, came up. . . . He had no gait, no station, no manner, rough, light-brown whiskers, a blue eye and rather a scrubby look withal. A crowd formed around him; men looked, stared at him, as if they were taking his likeness, and two generals were introduced . . .
>
> I joined the starers. I saw that the ordinary, scrubby-looking man, with a slightly seedy look, as if he was out of office and on half-pay and nothing to do but hang around the entry of Willard's, cigar in mouth, had a clear blue eye, and a look of resolution, as if he could not be trifled with, and an entire indifference to the

crowd about him. Straight nose, too. Still, to see him talking and smoking in the lower entry of Willard's, in that crowd, in such times—the generalissimo of our armies, on whom the destiny of the empire seemed to hang . . .

He gets over the ground queerly. He does not march, nor quite walk, but pitches along as if the next step would bring him on his nose.

This unlikely hero was the man all Washington had been buzzing about ever since it had been announced that he was to become the top general in the army. Everyone wanted to meet him, shake his hand, or merely get a glimpse of the conqueror of Vicksburg and the champion of Chattanooga. For his part, Grant was uncomfortable with all this attention. Reserved by nature, and downright shy when placed in situations out of his comfort zone, he surely wished to do in Washington what he never wanted to do on the battlefield: retreat.

Grant as lieutenant general and commander of all Union military forces is pictured at his headquarters in Virginia. (U.S. Army Military History Institute)

On March 9, the day after his arrival in the city, Grant went to the White House, where President Lincoln officially gave him his commission as lieutenant general. Grant's son was in attendance, along with the members of his staff who had come with him from Chattanooga. Lincoln was joined by his entire cabinet to receive the general and to witness the historic event.

Lincoln had been informed of Grant's "disinclination to speak in public," and before the ceremony began, the president gave him a sheet of paper on which he had written what he was going to say, as well as the reply the general should make. Lincoln said,

General Grant, the nation's appreciation of what you have done and its reliance upon you for what remains to be done in the existing great struggle, are now presented, with this commission constituting you lieutenant-general in the Army of the United States. With this high honor, devolves upon you, also, a corresponding responsibility. As the country herein trusts you, so under God, it will sustain you. I scarcely need to add, that, with, what I here speak for the nation, goes my own hearty personal concurrence.

Reading from the sheet, Grant replied,

Mr. President, I accept the commission, with gratitude for the high honor conferred. With the aid of the noble armies that have fought in so many fields for our common country, it will be my earnest endeavor not to disappoint your expectations. I feel the full weight of the responsibilities now devolving on me; and I know that if they are met, it will be due to those armies, and above all, to the favor of that Providence which leads both nations and men.

Grant now took charge of the affairs of all the Union armies. The timing was crucial. Grant was a hard fighter, and his command usually sustained high casualties in his campaigns. Through the first three years of war, the public had become hardened to the ever-increasing cost of the war. Casualty lists from battles such as Manassas and Ball's Bluff seemed like little more than brisk skirmishes when compared to the likes of Shiloh, Antietam, Gettysburg, and Chickamauga. Had Grant assumed control in the East in 1862, rather than 1864, it is probable that his style of fighting would have led to public outcry and that he would have been labeled as incompetent and relieved. By 1864, the public had become numbed to casualty lists in the tens of thousands, and those who supported the cause of the Union knew that tens of thousands more names would have to be added before the war could be brought to its conclusion.

The day after receiving his commission, Grant traveled to Brandy Station to visit the Army of the Potomac and make a call on General Meade. Meade was well aware of the efforts in Washington to replace him and evidently thought that Grant's visit signaled a change in command for the army. He told Grant that he could understand if he wished to have an officer who had served with him in the West take over the command and specifically mentioned Sherman. He further stated that the work before them was too important to be guided by personal feelings or ambitions and asserted that he would be happy to serve in any capacity Grant might see fit to assign him. Grant told Meade that he had no intention of replacing him and that Sherman was needed right where he was. Grant would accompany the army, but Meade would control its movements. Grant would decide matters of strategy, leaving Meade to implement all of the tactical details that arose. Grant returned to Washington on March 11 and left that night to meet with Sherman in Nashville. He had initially decided to return to the western theater after receiving his commission, but these plans had been changed. The eastern theater and the Army of the Potomac were where his talents were most needed, so he determined to remain there. Sherman was promoted to fill the vacancy in the West made by his departure, and General McPherson was elevated to take Sherman's place as commander of the Army of the Tennessee. Grant was meeting with Sherman to go over his plans for active operations once the spring campaign was begun.

The plan was simple in the extreme, but its simplicity was also its strength. Prior to the time Grant took overall command, Union armies had operated independent of one another, and there was virtually no concerted effort between them. The Confederates had been able to take advantage of this lack of cooperation and used their interior lines to shift forces back and forth to meet the enemy in threatened areas, while assuming a defensive posture in areas where the Federals were idle. Grant proposed a joint operation to be conducted in unison by all of the Federal armies. The Confederates would be pressured on all fronts simultaneously and would be denied the ability to fight the Union forces in detail. The vastly superior numbers of the Federal army could then be brought to bear to wear down the enemy. Southern armies were to be the objective, not Southern territory. What Grant proposed was essentially a war of attrition. Union forces would pin down the enemy in their sector of operations and would keep them engaged until they were overwhelmed and defeated by force of numbers. Casualties sustained in such a campaign would be extreme, but it was a foolproof way to end the war. For Grant, a practical man with a mechanic's mind, it seemed the obvious solution. While it would probably result in enormous losses, Grant reasoned that they would be no greater than if the war was allowed to continue on for years, fighting campaigns the way they had been conducted since 1861.

Sherman was instructed to drive for Atlanta, Georgia, making the Army of Tennessee and its new commander, General Joseph E. Johnston, his prime objective. General Nathaniel P. Banks was to operate against Mobile, Alabama, and then to cooperate with Sherman. Grant would return to the East, where he would oversee the campaign of the Army of the Potomac against Lee's Army of Northern Virginia. Major General Franz Sigel commanded the Department of West Virginia. He was to march his army down the Shenandoah Valley, engaging any enemy forces he found there. He was also to deny the enemy the use of the vast agricultural resources produced in the valley and prevent the corridor from being used as an invasion route to the North. Major General Benjamin Butler was in command of the Army of the James. His assignment was to take his force up the James River and operate against Richmond and Petersburg, Virginia. Major General George Crook was to move with a force of cavalry and artillery from his position in West Virginia to threaten the Virginia and Tennessee Railroad. According to Grant's plan, the Confederate armies would be assailed on all fronts at the same time and would not possibly be able to contend with the massive force arrayed against them. At some point, their defenses must crack, and Grant would be prepared to exploit the break. All Union forces were ordered to commence their portion of the plan as soon as the roads in their region were dry enough to allow active campaigning. Grant would be conducting his affairs in a manner that seemed unbelievable. All previous army commanders had been obliged to work closely with the civilian government. In many cases, political intrusion had contributed highly to defeat on the battlefield, but the military leaders were compelled to follow the directives of their civilian superiors and to gain permission for their anticipated movements from them. Grant was hampered by no such arrangement. The administration had become so confident in his abilities that it granted him authority to do what he felt best, without seeking permission. Grant's plan of campaign for the spring of 1864 was his own, and no other opinions were consulted. "I did not communicate my plans to the President," he would later write, "nor did I to the Secretary of War or to General Halleck." The government was granting the general complete freedom to fight the war as he thought best, something no other Union general had enjoyed during the war.

By April 27, Grant determined that weather conditions were appropriate to initiate his offensive in Virginia. May 4 was selected as the day the Army of the Potomac would advance against Lee's Confederates. Orders were sent to his various field commanders to begin their campaigns at the same time or as close as possible to it. On the appointed day, the Army of the Potomac crossed the Rapidan River and marched into the Wilderness, a 12-square-mile section of land near Chancellorsville. The Wilderness was aptly named. The region was sparsely populated as a result of the poor quality of its soil, the ruggedness of the landscape, and the thickness of its vegetation. Grant did not think that Lee would contest his movement through the Wilderness and planned to fight the decisive battle of the campaign once he had emerged from the tangled ground, where his 120,000-man army could be used to full advantage against Lee's 60,000 men on open ground. But Lee had other plans. Knowing that the rugged features of the Wilderness would limit the abilities of a large army to maneuver on the field, he planned to strike the Federals there, where Grant's superiority in numbers could not fully be brought to bear.

On May 5, the Army of the Potomac ran into Lee's army in the Wilderness, and a campaign that was to last six weeks and become the bloodiest military operation in American military history commenced. Onlookers reported that Grant seemed uncharacteristically nervous during his first encounter with Lee's famed Army of Northern Virginia. A member of his staff stated that his dress was immaculate—full uniform with coat buttoned and shoes shined—and for the first time that anyone could remember, he was even wearing gloves. As the sounds of battle reached his headquarters, he smoked cigars incessantly, and Horace Porter, a member of his staff, said that he smoked 20 of them during the course of the day. Grant seemed self-consumed and introspective. He talked little to those around him at the headquarters. Instead, he spent most of the day sitting under a tree, smoking his cigars and intently whittling on a piece of wood.

The first day's fighting at the Wilderness was marked by fierce charges and countercharges. The nature of the ground prohibited movements of large bodies of men, and the battle assumed the aspects of a soldier's fight, with smaller units fighting one another all over the field. The dense vegetation and the carpet of dried leaves on the ground created a peculiar circumstance in which fires were ignited from exploding artillery shells and the black powder discharges of the muskets. Soon, large areas of the Wilderness were burning, and the forest fires only added to the hellish nature of the fighting that was taking place. Pockets of men became trapped by the flames, and soldiers too severely wounded to flee could only watch as the fires burned steadily toward them. That night, when the fighting ended, the countryside was illuminated by the glow of the fires, and the cries of the wounded who could not escape them pierced the night and haunted the men of both armies.

The Army of the Potomac had been beaten, and many Union soldiers believed that Grant would retreat from the Wilderness to refit and reorganize. The soldiers of the Eastern army had not yet come to know the determination of the army's new commanding general. Grant had no intentions of giving ground. The battle was joined once more on May 6, and the fighting was even more desperate and bloody than the preceding day. By nightfall, the Union army had been fought to a standstill, and the Confederates had gained a tactical victory. The

Federals had lost more than 17,000 casualties, while inflicting only 11,000 on the enemy. During the night, Grant issued orders for the army to abandon its current positions. The men in the ranks had seen this all before. They had faced the Army of Northern Virginia for three years. The armies would come together for a battle, tremendous losses would be sustained, then each side would disengage to lick their wounds, reorganize, and prepare for the next bloodletting. As the men gathered their equipment, fell into ranks, and began to march away from the battlefield, they must surely have wondered how many more of these battles must be fought before one side or the other gained a clear advantage. Sullenly, they marched along until they realized that they were not retreating. Grant was not recrossing the Rapidan River. He was headed south, toward Richmond. There was to be no period of recuperation, no idle time to reorganize and prepare for the next campaign. Grant had seized hold of Robert E. Lee's Confederate army and he was not going to let go. Marching by Lee's right flank, Grant proposed to place his army between the Confederates and Richmond. The realization that they were going forward, not back, caused an eruption of spontaneous cheering among the marching troops. They had not been defeated in the Wilderness. They had merely been checked, but this fellow, Grant, didn't seem to let that interfere with his plans. Maybe the army had found a general who could lead them to victory.

General Lee anticipated Grant's movements and took steps to block them. When the Army of the Potomac arrived at the crossroads town of Spotsylvania Courthouse on May 9, it found the Confederates already there, behind prepared works, and ready to meet them. Union forces immediately probed the Southern lines looking for a weak spot, but none was to be found. Over the next few days, Grant ordered a number of frontal assaults to be made against the Confederate defenses. All of the attacks were thrown back with heavy losses. On May 11, Grant telegraphed General Halleck to report the progress of the army. "We have now ended the sixth day of very hard fighting," he wrote. "I propose to fight it out on this line if it takes all summer." The phrase excited the imagination of the Northern people in much the same way as his demand for unconditional surrender had at Fort Donelson. People in the North were sickened by the casualty lists that were already coming in from the Wilderness and Spotsylvania, but they took heart in the conviction that something of real importance was about to be accomplished.

On May 12, Grant launched a grand assault on a salient in the Confederate line known as the Mule Shoe. Twenty thousand men of Major General Winfield S. Hancock's II Corps advanced in the predawn hours to attack this critical position. In some of the fiercest fighting to take place during the war, Hancock's men were able to pierce the Confederate line. Some 4,000 enemy prisoners were captured, and it looked as if the Union troops were on the verge of splitting Lee's army in two and inflicting a terrible defeat on the Confederates. But General John B. Gordon led a counterattack to throw the Federals back. The fighting became even more bitterly contested, much of it hand-to-hand combat with bayonets and clubbed muskets. In the end, the Confederates were able to drive the Federals back and restore their defensive line. Thousands had fallen on the field of battle, but by the end of the day, the opposing armies were back in the respective positions they had occupied before the engagement began.

The contending armies sparred with one another for the next several days. Lee had constructed new defenses behind the Mule Shoe, and he withdrew his troops on that part of the line back to the new works. On May 18, Grant determined to test the strength of Lee's new defenses by ordering a frontal assault against them. The attack was easily repulsed, and the new works proved to be stronger and more formidable than the ones at the Mule Shoe. Grant saw that Lee's army could not be forced from these strong defenses, and it was futile to waste any more time or lives in attempting to do so. Over 31,000 casualties had been sustained by both armies thus far, with more than 18,000 of them being inflicted on the Union army. No positive results had come from all this bloodshed, and the Confederate army still defiantly blocked his way. If he could not force Lee's army out of its works, he would maneuver it out. As he had done at the Wilderness, Grant again ordered the army to march to the left, around Lee's right flank, in an attempt to interpose himself between the enemy and the Southern capital.

Lee once more anticipated Grant's movements and kept his army between the Federals and Richmond. The strategy of the campaign had been established: march to the left, around the Confederate flank and toward Richmond. By June 2, the armies had fought and maneuvered to within six miles of Richmond. Lee had taken up a strong position at a place called Cold Harbor, and Grant determined to end the martial dance by attacking the enemy with his entire army. At 4:30 on the morning of June 3, the Federal troops were ordered forward. Northern soldiers felt the attack was a suicide mission, and many of them wrote down their names and other personal information on small slips of paper and pinned them to their jackets so that their bodies could be identified after the battle. The soldiers were right. The attack lasted only about an hour and resulted in one of the most lopsided defeats of the war for the Union. During that hour, some 7,000 Union troops fell, while the Confederates suffered only 1,500 losses. Grant ordered Meade to prepare the army for another attack, but the officers and men had had enough. Brigadier General John Gibbon voiced the opinion of most when he stated, "We felt it was murder, not war." Meade reported to Grant that all of his corps commanders were against a resumption of the attack, and the soldiers were on the verge of mutiny. Grant bowed to the opinion of his subordinate generals. "The opinion of the corps commanders not being sanguine of success in case an assault is ordered, you may direct a suspension of further advance for the present," he instructed Meade.

The heavy losses were taking their toll on the Union army. In the six weeks that had passed since the first engagement at the Wilderness, the Federals had sustained losses that totaled approximately 55,000 men. Grant's army had lost about as many men as Lee had in his entire army at the beginning of the campaign. The elation that the soldiers in the ranks had felt when they first discovered they were not going to retreat following the Wilderness had been replaced by the conviction that none of them were going to survive this campaign. Brigadier John A. Rawlins, Grant's own chief-of-staff, bitterly protested against Grant's policy of continuous frontal attacks, calling it a "murderous policy of military incompetents." The people in the North echoed Rawlins's sentiments. They had expected the campaign to be costly, but the extreme casualty lists coming from the front were higher than anyone could have previously imagined. Grant's fitness for command was roundly debated, and he was commonly referred to as Grant the Butcher or just simply Butcher Grant. But the strategy of attrition was working. Grant constantly received reinforcements from the North to replace his losses, keeping his army at the level it had been when the campaign was begun. The Confederacy could not do the same for Lee. The South was running out of manpower, and there simply were no reserves available to replace Lee's losses.

Cold Harbor was to be the last major battle of the Overland Campaign of 1864. Grant decided to cross the James River with his army and approach Richmond from the south. By doing this, he could place his army in a position from which it could possibly cut off the two railroad lines over which Lee received his supplies. He would then be able to besiege the Confederates, as he had done at Vicksburg, or force them to abandon Richmond and retreat westward. When the vanguard of his army was across the river, he ordered it to advance against Petersburg without delay. Petersburg was approximately 20 miles south of Richmond, and its importance rested in the fact that the Weldon Railroad passed through it. If Grant could seize Petersburg, he could cut this line of communication and supply, leaving the Confederates with only the railroad coming from Danville to furnish their needs. Petersburg was lightly held by a small garrison under the command of General P.G.T. Beauregard. A general assault by the Union vanguard would certainly have resulted in the capture of the town, but no such assault was made. The soldiers in the army had become unnerved by the fighting of the past six weeks. When they saw Beauregard's defenders behind prepared works, they had flashbacks to the carnage of Cold Harbor and were hesitant to make what they thought might be another suicide charge. Instead, they began skirmishing with the enemy and probing his defenses. This hesitancy gave Lee time to shift a portion of his army south to reinforce Beauregard. With that accomplished, the Confederate position was too strong to be taken by assault.

Grant knew that he could not throw his army against the strong Southern defenses, so he brought up his heavy guns and prepared to lay siege to Richmond and Petersburg. His plan was to pin the Confederates where they were and not allow General Lee the opportunity to get his army out onto open ground, where he could maneuver and gain an advantage. The Federal army would then endeavor to extend to the left in an effort to cut the two railroads that served as Lee's lifelines. The end result was inevitable. Grant would either starve the Confederate army into submission, as he had at Vicksburg, or he would use his

two-to-one advantage in manpower to stretch the enemy line so thin
that it could be broken. As with all of his decisions, Grant's strategy
was simple and practical. The Confederates could not hope to win such
a contest, and it would only be a matter of time before Union arms pre-
vailed. Pemberton, at Vicksburg, had resisted for a month. Lee would
prove to be a much harder nut to crack, and he would hold Grant's
army at bay for nine months.

The overall military situation did not look favorable for those who
supported the Union cause in the summer and fall of 1864. Grant had
forced the Army of Northern Virginia to the very gates of Richmond,
but his offensive had stalled there, no closer to capturing the Southern capital or ending the war than General McClellan had been two
years earlier. To the Northern public, it looked like an unspeakable
waste of human lives, with precious little results to show for it. General
Sherman had engaged Joe Johnston's Army of Tennessee in northwest
Georgia and had pushed it through the state, in much the same manner as Grant had driven Lee through Virginia, but by August 1864,
his army was stalled on the outskirts of Atlanta. The Northern public
was becoming weary of the war, and many citizens were beginning to
come to the conclusion that the Southern Confederacy could not be
defeated on the battlefield. Support for Lincoln, and the Republican
administration, eroded. Unless some great victory could be won, it
looked as if Lincoln would be voted out of office in the fall elections. If
that happened, the war would be lost. The Democrats were campaigning on a platform of ending the fighting and suing for peace with the
Confederacy, and the nation would be permanently divided if they won
the elections. Lincoln needed a victory on the battlefield to stay in
office. That victory was not going to come from Virginia, where Grant
appeared to be stalemated by Lee. It came instead from Georgia, where
the Confederate high command made a crucial mistake that destroyed
any chance of Southern independence.

General Joe Johnston had conducted a masterful defensive campaign against Sherman in Georgia. He had given ground, to be sure,
but he had managed to blunt every effort Sherman made to destroy his
army or to get between him and Atlanta. By July, he had fallen back to
the outskirts of the city. Atlanta boasted some of the strongest fortifications to be found in America, and Johnston was sure that he could in-

duce Sherman into battering his army to pieces in trying to take them. But at this juncture, fate intervened to favor the cause of the Union. President Jefferson Davis was not a supporter of Johnston. The two had been feuding in public since 1861, when Johnston took offense to his placement on the roll of full Confederate generals of the army. Davis had been concerned over Johnston's numerous withdrawals and had been urging the general to fight a decisive battle before he was pushed back to Atlanta. When Johnston's army reached the environs of the city without fighting a climactic battle, Davis finally had enough.

On July 17, 1864, Johnston was relieved of command and replaced by General John Bell Hood. Hood was known as one of the most aggressive combat commanders in the Confederate army. An offensive-minded leader, Hood gave little thought to the defensive measure Johnston had adopted that had thus far prevented the Federals from achieving their goal. Hood chose to attack the Union army, instead of inducing it to attack him behind his strong works. In three separate battles, he marched his army out into the open and threw it against Sherman's veterans. Each assault ended in a costly repulse for the Confederates, and by the time the three battles were over, Hood no longer had enough men left in his army to prevent Sherman from capturing Atlanta. On September 1, Hood ordered the evacuation of the city, and Sherman's forces marched into Atlanta the following day. Atlanta was won. The stalemate was broken. The Northern public once more took heart that the war could be brought to a successful conclusion. In the end, Lincoln was sustained at the polls, and his reelection guaranteed that the war would be persecuted to the bitter end.

Back in Virginia, the siege of Petersburg and Richmond was dragging on. It was not a siege in the conventional sense of the word, however. Neither city was surrounded, as Vicksburg had been. Neither were the Confederate forces cut off from their source of supplies. What actually took place was trench warfare, a foreshadowing of the tremendous struggle that would take place half a century later in World War I. The opposing sides confronted one another with daily artillery barrages, sniper fire, and frequent sorties to probe for weaknesses. Grant enjoyed more than a two-to-one superiority in manpower, but Lee was able to thwart his efforts and keep him out of Richmond. Grant continued to extend his line to the left, searching for a way to cut the railroads and force Lee to abandon his defenses. By the time the siege was ended, the Union line would stretch for over 30 miles, from the eastern outskirts of Richmond to the south of Petersburg. As fall gave way to winter, it seemed as if there would be no way to break the stalemate at Richmond and Petersburg.

The year 1865 promised to be the decisive year of the war, and the Union armies seemed poised to deliver the fateful blow that would end the conflict and force the capitulation of the Southern Confederacy. In the West, Sherman had left Atlanta and conducted his famed March to the Sea, splitting the Confederacy in two and capturing the port city of Savannah in December. He then turned north, marching his army through the Carolinas, intent on joining with Grant to crush the Army of Northern Virginia for good. In Tennessee, General Thomas met John Bell Hood at the Battle of Nashville. Thomas crushed Hood in one of the most decisive victories in all of military history, and the once proud Army of Tennessee all but ceased to exist. With the coming of the spring campaign season, all eyes were now on Virginia and the death struggle taking place between Lee and Grant.

A contemporary drawing shows the trench warfare Grant's forces engaged in for over nine months in the lines around Richmond and Petersburg. (U.S. Army Military History Institute)

The Army of the Potomac had been successful in cutting a portion of the Weldon Railroad the previous August, and Grant planned to operate against the one remaining source of supplies for Lee as soon as the roads had dried sufficiently to put his army in motion. On March 24, Grant issued orders that would cause his line to "extend out west toward Five Forks, the object being to get into a position from which we could strike the South Side Railroad and ultimately the Danville Railroad." By March 31, Union forces, under the command of Major General Philip Sheridan, had reached the vicinity of Five Forks. General George E. Pickett, of Gettysburg fame, was in command of the 9,200 Confederate troops assigned to protect the place. On April 1, Sheridan launched his attack. The initial Federal assault was poorly delivered, but the Confederate defense was hampered by a lack of leadership. When the Federal attack was made, General Pickett was two miles away, enjoying a shad bake with a couple other general officers. An acoustic shadow prevented him from hearing the sounds of the battle, which was being fought by subordinate officers of his command. By the time Pickett learned what was taking place, Sheridan had taken personal charge of events and led a charge that broke the left flank of the Confederate line. When Pickett reached the field, there was little he could do but watch as the survivors of his command retreated in confusion. Sheridan had inflicted almost 3,000 casualties on Pickett's command, while suffering only 830 himself. More importantly, he had placed his command in a position to cut off the South Side Railroad.

General Lee realized the magnitude of the defeat at Five Forks. Grant now had the ability to seize his remaining rail lifeline, and he had forces in place that would prevent a retreat of the Army of Northern Virginia to the south. The outcome was now certain. If Lee remained where he was, Grant would cut off his supplies and starve his army into submission. His only option was to abandon Richmond and Petersburg and retreat to the west, in hopes of being able to join forces with General Joe Johnston's makeshift army that had recently been defeated by Sherman at the Battle of Bentonville, North Carolina. Lee called on President Davis to inform him of his decision and the need to transfer the Confederate government out of Richmond. On April 2, Lee pulled his army out of its defensive works and pointed it westward. The following day, Union forces took possession of both Petersburg and

Richmond. They had been held at bay for more than nine months, but they had finally captured the prize. Grant realized that he had gained only a partial victory, however. It would not be complete until the Army of Northern Virginia was captured or destroyed.

On April 3, Grant entered Petersburg accompanied by General Meade. He did not stop to enjoy the victory he had thus far won. "I was sure Lee was trying to make his escape, and I wanted to push immediately in pursuit," he wrote. As he looked at the rear guard of the retreating Confederate army, Grant stated, "I hoped to capture them soon." Grant correctly guessed that Lee would make for Danville. Meade suggested that the Federal army follow Lee, but Grant stated emphatically, "We did not want to follow him; we wanted to get ahead of him and cut him off." It would now become a footrace. Grant wanted to get a blocking force on the Danville Railroad where it crossed the Appomattox River, and he ordered the advance of his army to proceed to that point with all haste. Federal cavalry was able to get to the south of Lee's retreating army, effectively blocking the way to Danville. The only route open to the Confederate army was to continue west, toward Lynchburg. Lee's army was desperately short of food, and arrangements had been made for a large quantity of rations to be sent to Farmville.

On April 6, Sheridan's cavalry, supported by the infantry of the 2nd and 6th Corps, cut off a fourth of the retreating Confederate army at Sayler's Creek. Lieutenant General Richard Ewell had the divisions of Custis Lee and Joseph Kershaw with him, but they were no match for the Union forces arrayed against them. The Confederates tried to cut their way out of the trap but to no avail. Almost 8,000 men were forced to surrender, including nine general officers. On April 7, the armies clashed in a minor affair at Farmville, but the main result was that the Confederates were forced to send their trains of provisions ahead to keep them from falling into enemy hands, without being able to unload any of the badly needed supplies. On that same day, General Sheridan learned that seven trains of supplies and forage were waiting for Lee at Appomattox, farther to the west. Sheridan ordered his cavalry to make a forced march to get there before Lee and capture the trains. The trap was closing on Lee and his army. Grant knew it, and he was sure that Lee knew it as well. Grant decided to contact Lee to open a correspondence on the subject of the possible surrender of his army. He wrote Lee a letter stating,

> The results of the last week must convince you of the hopelessness of further resistance on the part of the Army of Northern Virginia in this struggle. I feel that it is so, and regard it as my duty to shift from myself the responsibility of any further effusion of blood, by asking of you the surrender of that portion of the Confederate States army known as the Army of Northern Virginia.

Lee knew that his situation was desperate, but he was not yet convinced that it was hopeless. He still felt there was a chance his men could escape the pursuit, but he was willing to listen to Grant's proposal. On the evening of April 7, he replied to Grant's letter, informing the general, "I have received your note of this day. Though not entertaining the opinion you express on the hopelessness of further resistance on the part of the Army of Northern Virginia, I reciprocate your desire to avoid the useless effusion of blood, and therefore before considering your proposition, ask the terms you will offer on condition of its surrender."

Grant felt that Lee was trying to buy time, but the following morning he wrote another letter, outlining his basic surrender demands.

> Your note of last evening in reply to mine of the same date, asking the condition on which I will accept the surrender of the Army of Northern Virginia is just received. In reply I would say that, peace being my great desire, there is but one condition I would insist upon, namely: that the men and officers surrendered shall be disqualified from taking up arms again against the Government of the United States until properly exchanged. I will meet you, or will designate officers to meet any officers you may name for the same purpose, at any point agreeable to you, for the purpose of arranging definitely the terms upon which the surrender of the Army of Northern Virginia will be received.

On the night of April 8, a division of Sheridan's cavalry under the command of General George Armstrong Custer reached Appomattox

Station. They were now in front of Lee's army, blocking his westward retreat. When the Confederates discovered the blue-clad troopers on the morning of April 9, they attacked in an effort to push them out of the way. The attack was made by General John B. Gordon's depleted corps, supported by Fitzhugh Lee's cavalry. The Confederates initially drove the Union troopers back, but the timely arrival on the field of the 5th Corps sealed the fate of the Southern army. Lee was now virtually surrounded. His army was out in the open without fortifications and facing an enemy that outnumbered him by almost four to one. Lee did the only thing he could do: he sent word to Grant that he wished to discuss the terms of surrender.

Grant had spent the previous night some distance behind the main body of the army. He had been experiencing a severe headache and had stopped at a farmhouse, where he soaked his feet and applied mustard plants to his wrists and neck in hopes of relieving the pain. He was already on his way to the front the next morning, however, when he received word that Lee had raised the white flag and asked for a truce. Grant made his way for Sheridan's position, in front of the Confederate army, where he inquired as to the location of Lee. He was informed that Lee was in Appomattox Court House, at the home of Wilmer McLean. McLean had sold his home in Manassas following the first battle of the war and had moved west in hopes of escaping the conflict. But the war had followed him, and its final chapter in the East would be enacted in his parlor. As for the events that transpired during the surrender proceedings, Grant's own words will tell the story.

> When I left camp that morning I had not expected so soon the result that was taking place, and consequently was in rough garb. I was without a sword, as I usually was when on horseback on the field, and wore a soldier's blouse for a coat, with the shoulder straps of my rank to indicate to the army who I was. When I went into the house I found General Lee. We greeted each other, and after shaking hands took our seats. I had my staff with me, a good portion of whom were in the room during the whole of the interview.
>
> What General Lee's feelings were I do not know. As he was a man of much dignity, with an impassable face, it was impossible to

say whether he felt inwardly glad that the end had finally come, or felt sad over the result, and was too manly to show it. Whatever his feelings, they were entirely concealed from my observation; but my own feelings, which had been quite jubilant on the receipt of his letter, were sad and depressed. I felt like anything rather than rejoicing at the downfall of a foe who had fought so long and valiantly, and had suffered so much for a cause, though that cause was, I believe, one of the worst for which a people ever fought, and one for which there was the least excuse. I do not question, however, the sincerity of the great mass of those who were opposed to us.

General Lee was dressed in a full uniform which was entirely new, and was wearing a sword of considerable value, very likely the sword which had been presented by the State of Virginia; at all events, it was an entirely different sword from the one that would ordinarily be worn in the field. In my rough traveling suit, the uniform of a private with the straps of a lieutenant general, I must have contrasted very strangely with a man so handsomely dressed, six feet high and of faultless form. But this was not a matter that I thought of until afterwards.

We soon fell into a conversation about old army times. He remarked that he remembered me very well in the old army; and I told him that as a matter of course I remembered him perfectly, but from the difference in our rank and years (there being about sixteen years' difference in our ages), I had thought it very likely that I had not attracted his attention sufficiently to be remembered by him after such a long interval. Our conversation grew so pleasant that I almost forgot the object of our meeting. After the conversation had run on in this style for some time, General Lee called my attention to the object of our meeting and said that he had asked for this interview for the purpose of getting from me the terms I proposed to give his army. I said that I meant merely that his army should lay down their arms, not to take them up again during the continuance of the war unless duly and properly exchanged. He said that he had so understood my letter.

Then we gradually fell off again into conversation about matters foreign to the subject which had brought us together. This

continued for some little time, when General Lee again inter-
rupted the course of the conversation by suggesting that the terms
I proposed to give his army ought to be written out. I called to
General [Ely S.] Parker, secretary on my staff, for writing materi-
als, and commenced writing out the following terms:

> Gen.: In accordance with the substance of my letter to you
> of the 8th, inst., I propose to receive the surrender of the
> Army of N. Va. On the following terms, to wit: Rolls of all
> the officers and men to be made in duplicate. One copy to
> be given to an officer designated by me, the other to be re-
> tained by such officer or officers as you may designate. The
> officers to give their individual paroles not to take up arms
> against the Government of the United States until properly
> exchanged, and each company or regimental commander
> sign a like parole for the men of their commands. The arms,
> artillery and public property to be parked and stacked, and
> turned over to the officer appointed by me to receive them.
> This will not embrace the side-arms of the officers, nor their
> private horses or baggage. This done, each officer and man
> will be allowed to return to their homes, not to be disturbed
> by United States authority so long as they observe their pa-
> roles and the laws in force where they may reside.

Lee read the terms and remarked that the part allowing the officers
to keep their sidearms and private property would be happily received.
He then sought the only concession asked of Grant. Explaining that
Confederate soldiers serving in the cavalry and artillery provided their
own horses, instead of having them issued by the government, he inquired as to whether something could be done to allow them to keep
their property. Grant thought about it for a second and then stated
that the U.S. government did not want the animals. Because most
of the soldiers in Lee's army were farmers, they would need them to put
in a crop, so any soldier in the Army of Northern Virginia who claimed
to own a horse or mule would be allowed to take it with him following the surrender. Grant added this condition to the terms of surrender, at which time Lee formally wrote out his acceptance. Copies were
made of both documents, and while they were being penned, Grant

introduced the members of his staff. Each general designated officers to facilitate the surrender, and Lee took his leave to return to his own lines.

Grant sent a telegraph to Washington informing the administration that "General Lee surrendered the Army of Northern Virginia this afternoon on terms proposed by myself. The accompanying additional correspondence will show the conditions fully." Word of the surrender quickly spread through the ranks of both armies. In the Union camps, it was met with unbridled elation and enthusiasm. In the Confederate camps, it was met with heartbroken tears. Grant said, "When news of the surrender first reached our lines our men commenced firing a salute of a hundred guns in honor of the victory. I at once sent word, however, to have it stopped. The Confederates were now our prisoners, and we did not want to exult over their downfall."

Grant's manly consideration for his vanquished foes was commendable, but there was much reason for celebration on the part of the Union troops. For all intents and purposes, the war was over. True, Joe

An artist's rendition of the surrender ceremonies at Appomattox Court House, Virginia, when Grant received the surrender of Robert E. Lee's Army of Northern Virginia appears here. Regrettably, there were no photographers in attendance to capture the event for posterity. (U.S. Army Military History Institute)

Johnston's army was still in the field in North Carolina, but it was being pursued by Sherman and was expected to capitulate shortly. The only other military forces the Confederacy had in the field were mainly small formations that could offer only local resistance and would surely lay down their arms once news of the surrender of their two principle armies reached them. Though it would take until June before the last Confederate soldiers surrendered and signed their paroles, the surrender at Appomattox Court House signaled the end of the Confederacy and the conclusion of the war. Grant was the hero of the day and was hailed as the architect of the victory. His name was mentioned along with Lincoln's as being the savior of the Union. He had achieved the pinnacle of his military success and ensured his place in the nation's history as one of its greatest military leaders.

Chapter 10

A WARRIOR TO THE END

Following the surrender at Appomattox, Grant traveled to Washington to meet with President Lincoln and the civilian authorities. On April 14, he was a guest at Lincoln's cabinet meeting, at which the president expressed his hopes that the nation could be reunited without persecution or resentments. Lincoln opposed punitive measures or confiscation of any private property of Southerners. He also opposed universal suffrage for blacks, except those who could read and write and had served in the military. He felt that the states should regulate suffrage themselves, feeling that the question was not within the authority of the Federal government. Grant listened attentively to the president's words and fully understood the sentiment they expressed.

Julia had accompanied Grant to the capital, and Lincoln extended an invitation to his top general and his wife to accompany him and Mary Todd for a social outing that evening. Lincoln planned to attend Ford's Theater to see a play and wanted Grant to come along. The general declined the offer, however. He informed Lincoln that his children were attending school in Burlington, New Jersey, and he had not seen them in a while. If he got all of his work completed, he and Julia intended to leave that evening for a long-overdue family reunion.

Grant had reached Philadelphia when he was met with the news of Lincoln's assassination. Secretary Seward had also been attacked and was rumored to be dead. Popular speculation had it that Vice President Andrew Johnson had also been assassinated. Grant was ordered to return to Washington immediately.

> Grant remembered that he was overcome by the news, especially the assassination of the President. I knew his goodness of heart, his generosity, his yielding disposition, his desire to have everybody happy, and above all his desire to see all the people of the United States enter again upon the full privileges of citizenship with equality among all. I knew also the feeling that Mr. Johnson had expressed in speeches and conversation against the Southern people, and I feared that his course towards them would be such as to repel, and make them unwilling citizens; and if they became such they would remain so for a long while. I felt that reconstruction had been set back, no telling how far.

Grant's perception of the change in political policy occasioned by Lincoln's death was prophetically accurate. The radical portion of the Republican Party had been displeased with Lincoln's treatment of the South for some time now. They favored harsh methods of reconstruction that would punish the South for its role in creating the war and would destroy all vestiges of Southern institutions and culture. At a political caucus held the day after Lincoln's death, the prevailing sentiment reported was one of shock and surprise but not of grief. Lincoln's views on reconstruction were "as distasteful as possible to Radical Republicans," and most in attendance felt that "the accession of Johnson would prove a Godsend to the country." Many radical Republicans would have agreed with Albert S. Hunt, a Methodist minister, when he said, "Wherever Lincoln has erred it has been on the side of mercy . . . and there are those who listen to me to-day who think that Providence has permitted this calamity to befall us that a sterner hand might rule in our national affairs."

Grant and Lincoln had shared similar views in regard to the treatment of the Southern states once the war was ended. The leniency of the surrender terms given to Lee shows that Grant agreed with Lincoln's policy to "let them up easy" as the proper way to reunite the country. Now he would have to work with a different commander-in-chief, whose political agenda was far different from his predecessor. Grant's first official duty under Johnson would be to reprimand his old friend and subordinate: William T. Sherman.

General Joseph E. Johnston had contacted Sherman on April 14 requesting a truce so that the two commanders could discuss terms of surrender for Johnston's army. Sherman agreed and set the date for the meeting on April 17. Sherman was boarding a train to travel to Durham for his meeting on the morning of the 17th when he received a telegraph informing him of Lincoln's assassination three days earlier. He decided to keep his appointment with Johnston, though, and made his way to the meeting place, a little farmhouse owned by the Bennett family. When Sherman informed Johnston and his officers of the news he had just received, it seemed to affect the Confederate officers as genuinely as it did the officers on Sherman's own staff. Johnston and his officers made forceful denunciations of the act and expressed the belief that Lincoln's loss was as much a tragedy to the South as it was to the North. Without Lincoln in charge, the Southerners feared that the process of reunification would be harsh and prolonged. Sherman was convinced that the Confederates were sincere and that Booth and his coconspirators had acted on their own and not as part of any official conspiracy. He therefore concluded to move forward with the surrender talks.

So much time was spent discussing Lincoln's death and its possible ramifications on the peace process that the day was growing late when the terms of surrender were finally brought up. It was decided, therefore, that the two generals would meet again the next day, at the same place, to conclude their discussions. Johnston sought to gain better terms than had been given to Lee. He felt that the difference in circumstances between his army and Lee's justified such a request. Lee had been cut off and surrounded. Johnston's army had been able to place a distance of 80 miles between it and Sherman's army. It still had room to maneuver and could march south and continue the war for an unspecified period of time. He was not requesting terms of surrender because he felt his army was in a hopeless position but was doing so because he believed the Confederacy to be beaten and wished to

prevent any further sacrifice of life for a lost cause. Also, General John
Breckinridge, the current secretary of war for the Confederacy, was with
Johnston and offered to negotiate the surrender of all Confederate
forces still in the field.

When Sherman and Johnston met on April 18, Johnston pressed
his case, and Sherman seemed agreeable to granting concessions.
Sherman, as Grant, was intimate with the desires of Lincoln to reunite the country in a fair and judicious manner, and he felt that
Breckinridge's offer to negotiate for all Confederate forces would bring
the war to a close and was therefore worth making some concessions.
Sherman's terms were not only far more lenient than Grant's had been;
they entered into areas of diplomacy and political policy that he had
no authority to discuss. Sherman agreed to allow the Confederate soldiers to return home with their weapons, which would be deposited
in their various state arsenals. He guaranteed all political rights to the
Confederates and even went so far as to promise that state legislatures
and courts could resume their work so long as their members took an
oath of allegiance to the Federal government. When Sherman sent
the details of his surrender terms to President Johnson and Secretary
Stanton, it caused such a furor that Sherman was even accused of being
a traitor. When these accusations were made to Grant, he "grew in-
dignant, and gave free expression to his opposition to an attempt to
stigmatize an officer whose acts throughout all his career gave ample
contradiction to the charge that he was actuated by unworthy motives."
Nonetheless, Grant was ordered to travel to North Carolina himself
to relieve Sherman and take over the surrender negotiations.

Grant left Washington on the morning of April 22, and by the 24th,
he had arrived at Sherman's headquarters. Grant's handling of the
situation showed that he was not only a friend to Sherman but a states-
man and diplomat as well.

> When I arrived I went to Sherman's headquarters, and we were at
> once closeted together. I showed him the instructions and orders
> under which I visited him. I told him that I wanted him to notify
> General Johnston that the terms which they had conditionally
> agreed upon had not been approved in Washington, and that he
> was authorized to offer the same terms I had given General Lee.

I sent Sherman to do this himself. I did not wish the knowledge of my presence to be known to the army generally; so I left it to Sherman to negotiate the terms of the surrender solely by himself, and without the enemy knowing that I was anywhere near the field. As soon as possible I started to get away, to leave Sherman quite free and untrammeled.

Sherman contacted Johnston, and a meeting was set for April 26. Johnston wished to get more from Sherman than Grant had given Lee, but Sherman was now bound by strict guidelines. At length, Johnston agreed, the terms of surrender were signed, and Johnston's 31,000 men became noncombatants. Grant's handling of the situation had not only prevented Sherman from being disgraced; it had given him the opportunity to redeem himself with the administration. More than that, it showed Grant's personal disdain for the heavy-handed methods of the radicals. Though he had no way of knowing it, within a few months President Johnson would mellow in his treatment of the South to the point of being magnanimous. He would become the defender not only of the South but of the Constitution as well and would be the most hated man in America, so far as the radicals were concerned.

Grant spent the remainder of the year 1865 overseeing the administration of the army, conducting military affairs, and receiving the praise of a grateful nation. When he traveled to Galena, he found that the sidewalk he had quipped about as being his only political agenda had already been built. He also found that he was the owner of one of the nicest houses in town. The people of Galena had raised $16,000, through subscription, and had used the money to buy their most famous citizen a fully furnished house. The citizens of Philadelphia presented Grant with a house that was even more luxurious than the Galena residence, and New York City gave him $100,000 in cash. Boston presented him with a library valued at $5,000, and gifts of horses came from all over the country. He was the toast of the nation, and everyone wanted to meet him. In 1866, Congress approved a measure to revive the rank of full general in the U.S. Army, and it was given to Grant in recognition of his services to the country.

In November 1865, President Johnson sent Grant on a fact-finding mission through the South. Johnson was interested in obtaining

information concerning the sentiments of the Southern people in regard to Reconstruction. Grant spent only 10 days making his Southern
tour, but his report was all that Johnson could have hoped for. "I am
satisfied that the mass of thinking men of the South accept the present
situation of affairs in good faith," Grant said.

> My observations lead me to the conclusion that the citizens of the
> Southern states are anxious to return to self-government within
> the Union as soon as possible; that while reconstructing they want
> and require protection from the government; and that they are
> in earnest in wishing to do what is required by the government,
> not humiliating to them as citizens, and that if such a course was
> pointed out they would pursue it in good faith.

Johnson favored a speedy reinstatement of the Southern states to
their former place in the Union. The radical Republicans in Congress
were opposed to this. They stated that, by virtue of their leaving the
Union, the Southern states no longer existed as functioning bodies.
The radicals called for military governors to be appointed in the conquered Southern territories. They also advocated that blacks in the
South be given the vote while any white man having anything to do
with the recent rebellion be denied the franchise. Congress wanted to
punish the Southern people for the war, and it did not want to readmit
any Southern state to the Union until that state had been "cleansed"
of all things Southern. Radical Republican leaders even wanted to try
all the leaders of the Confederacy for treason and have them executed.
Johnson and Congress were fundamentally opposed in philosophy, and
it would lead to a power struggle between the nation's executive and
legislative branches of government, the likes of which the country had
never before seen.

The Fourteenth Amendment to the Constitution had been passed
by Congress, and it became a main point of political contention in
the nation. The amendment granted citizenship to the ex-slaves of the
South. It allowed the individual states to determine the qualifications
for allowing the blacks within their states to vote. Lastly, it disenfran-
chised ex-Confederates and denied them from holding any Federal of-
fices. The amendment was met with resentment and resistance in the

South, where its ratification was made a condition of readmittance into the Union. Wrangling over its adoption would last for the next few years, with the measure not being ratified until July 1868.

In the meantime, President Johnson was trying to blunt the punitive measures of Congress as he pursued his own policies of Reconstruction. He constantly vetoed bills from the radical Republicans that were placed before him, only to have them passed into law by a two-thirds' majority of Congress. Hoping to take his case to the people, Johnson set out on a tour of the country to speak to the people directly in a series of town meetings. The president took with him Grant and Admiral David Farragut in an effort to impress the people. The tour was a dismal failure and showed Johnson's lack of popularity with the voters. This only served to embolden the radicals, and in December 1866, Congress passed a bill known as the Reconstruction Act. This act eliminated the state governments that had thus far been established by Johnson and replaced them with five military departments, each to be commanded by a general of the army. That same day, Congress passed another bill stripping Johnson of his authority as commander-in-chief by demanding that any contact of the president with the army had to go through the commanding general, Grant. The radicals had been doing their best to influence Grant and bring him into the fold, and by the end of 1866, they were confident that their mission had been accomplished. Grant and Johnson had both gone full circle. Johnson, the liberal and darling of the radicals, had become conservative. Grant, the conservative, had shifted his political ideologies to the side of the radicals and was soon to become their standard-bearer. The era of Presidential Reconstruction was coming to a close, and Radical Reconstruction was about to begin.

In March 1867, Congress passed the Tenure of Office Act. This bill made it impossible for the president to remove from office any official who had been ratified by the Senate and made Senate approval mandatory for any such dismissal. Congress passed this legislation to keep Johnson from removing radical appointees and replacing them with moderate or conservative politicians. The law received its first test in the case of Secretary of War Edwin Stanton. Stanton was a fiery radical and a fierce opponent of everything Johnson stood for. The president sought to remove this political enemy from the cabinet and removed him from office while Congress was in recess. Johnson, still believing Grant to be a political ally, appointed the general as secretary of war ad interim.

But Grant's shift to the radicals was now complete. Secretary of the Navy Gideon Welles recorded in his diary, "General Grant has become severely afflicted with the Presidential disease, and it warps his judgment, which is not very intelligent or enlightened at best. He is less sound on great and fundamental principles, and vastly less informed, then I had supposed possible for a man of his opportunities." In an interview with Welles, Grant expounded on his political ideas, all of which were based on the prevailing radical dogma. He said that he looked upon the Southern states as conquered territory, having no rights within the framework of the Federal government. It was the prerogative of Congress, he maintained, to decide all matters regarding the formation of state governments in the South, the readmittance of those states, and such far-ranging issues as who could and could not vote within their borders. Welles was stunned by this revelation. "That, I told him was not only a virtual dissolution of the Union, but an abandonment of our republican federal system. It was establishing a central power, which could control and destroy—a power above and beyond the Constitution."

When Congress reconvened, its first order of business was to address the situation with Stanton. The secretary was ordered to be reinstated to his post, and Grant complied by vacating the office and allowing Stanton to walk in. Johnson felt betrayed. The president knew that Congress would oppose his removal of Stanton and try to overturn his action based on the Tenure of Office Act. Johnson thought that the act was unconstitutional and planned to test it by having it reviewed by the Supreme Court. The only way this could take place, however, was if Grant retained the post of secretary of war, causing Stanton to sue for reinstatement. Johnson said all the details had been discussed with Grant, and he had been in accordance. By simply removing himself from office and allowing Stanton to resume control without opposition, Grant had ruined Johnson's plan and had destroyed any possibility to test the Tenure of Office Act before the Supreme Court. Johnson felt that Grant had gone back on his word and accused him publically of political intrigue. Tension between Grant and Johnson now reached its climax. Grant took offense to Johnson's public condemnation and issued a broadside of his own in response. He stated that he had never given Johnson any reason to believe that he would disobey an order of Congress, which he felt was the final authority in the matter. He accused the president of assailing his "honor as a soldier and integrity as a man" and regarded the "whole matter from beginning to end as an attempt to involve me in a resistance of law for which you hesitated to assume the responsibility, and thus destroy my character before the country." When Grant attended a meeting of the cabinet on January 14, 1868, he attempted to explain his actions and justify his methods. He told those assembled that it had been his intention to remove himself from the office so that Johnson could appoint some other person to test the law, but he had been so occupied with military matters that the issue had come to its conclusion before he had a chance to do so. His explanation was not widely accepted, as few thought that so important an action could have slipped his mind.

Johnson did make another appointment to the office of secretary of state. General Lorenzo Thomas was chosen to replace Stanton, but the change could not take place. Stanton barricaded himself in his office and refused to leave. Congress entered the fray, on behalf of Stanton, by bringing charges against Johnson for his failure to observe the Tenure of Office Act and calling for his impeachment. The rift between Grant and Johnson caused the general to personally visit a number of senators in an effort to influence their votes against the president. In the end, Johnson would survive the impeachment proceedings by a single vote, but his ability to be a factor in the nation's politics was destroyed.

On May 20, 1868, the Republican Party met in Chicago to hold its national convention. The delegates adopted a platform that included adoption of congressional Reconstruction, pensions for Union veterans who had fought in the late war, and encouragement of foreign immigration. The delegates took the opportunity to publically mourn the death of President Lincoln and lashed out vehemently against Johnson and his policies. John Logan, a Congressman from Illinois and former Union general, rose to nominate Ulysses S. Grant as the Republican candidate for president in the fall election. The nomination was passed in a unanimous vote on the first ballot. The next order of business was the selection of a vice presidential candidate. Benjamin Wade, Henry Wilson, and Schuyler Colfax were the leading contenders for the position. On the sixth ballot, Colfax received the necessary majority of votes, and the Republican ticket for the 1868 election was set. Grant had declined to attend the convention. He was home in Galena when news reached him of his nomination. An observer said he received the information with the same stoic nature that had come to typify his command during the war: "There was no shade of exultation or agitation on his face, not a flush on his cheek, nor a flash in his eye."

The Democrats held their convention in New York City in July. They were not nearly as unified in their support of a presidential nominee, and it took 22 ballots before Horatio Seymour was chosen as their standard-bearer. The convention then selected Francis P. Blair Jr. to be Seymour's vice presidential running mate. The Democrats claimed that theirs was the only party that could bind the nation's wounds and bring about a peaceful reconciliation of the states. Grant was portrayed as a drunken, Negro-loving tyrant, and Colfax, who had previously been a member of the Nativist Party, was depicted as being anti-Catholic.

Grant followed the traditional custom in presidential elections and remained at home, leaving the campaigning to others. Various political clubs, such as the Tanners and the Boys in Blue, sprang up to support Grant and forward the Republican banner. Democrats were accused of supporting slavery, secession, and all efforts to thwart the Union war effort. Seymour was blamed as being an instigator of the New York City Draft Riots that had taken place in 1863, and affiliation with the Peace Party led to insinuations that he had committed treason. In order to combat the allegations of Grant's excessive drinking, Republicans claimed that Blair was a drunkard. Ultimately, it would be Grant's fame as a war hero and the public popularity rising from his military acclaim that would overshadow all political platforms and all campaign accusations.

Seymour did not observe the custom of allowing others to campaign for him. Instead, he took to the road to make a series of stump speeches for his election, making stops in Buffalo, Philadelphia, Pittsburgh,

Cleveland, Columbus, Detroit, Indianapolis, and Chicago. His campaign tour showed that Seymour enjoyed unexpected strength with the voters and promised that the election would be a closely contested affair. In the November election, Grant won the presidency by an overwhelming electoral count of 214 to 80, but the results of the electoral college do not tell the entire story. Grant's margin of victory in the popular vote was just 309,000, a fact that was a severe disappointment to campaign managers. The vote was painfully close in a number of key states, and in several contests, victory had been gained because blacks had voted as a block for Grant while many of their white counterparts had been denied the right to vote. Nonetheless, on March 4, 1869, Grant took the oath of office and became president. His inauguration was somewhat conspicuous because of the absence of the outgoing executive, Andrew Johnson. Grant was still harboring bitter feelings toward Johnson and refused to allow him to ride in the carriage to the inauguration ceremonies. In many ways, it was a childish action, but it was consistent with the focus and single-purpose approach Grant had displayed throughout his life. Johnson had earned his enmity, and neither the solemnity of the moment nor the distinguished nature of his office would cause the president-elect to waver from the animosity he felt toward him.

Grant's first order of business as president was to form his cabinet. Members of the radical Republican faction were eager to learn of his intended appointments, though they were chagrined that they had not been consulted in making the selections. Grant realized that his immense popularity as a war hero had been the primary reason for both his nomination and his election, and he seemed to view the presidency as some sort of reward for his service to the nation, rather than an office of grave responsibility. He not only snubbed the radical Republicans by not involving them in the decision-making process to select cabinet members; he ignored the role they had played in securing his victory in the election by not naming any of the leading members to a post. Instead, he formed his cabinet from men he liked or admired personally, and in many cases, Grant's friendship was their only qualification for the job. John Bigelow, a New York politician, said that Grant seemed to have no comprehension of political forces, that "his

Cabinet are merely staff officers, selected apparently out of motives of gratitude or for pecuniary favors received from them. His relatives and other friends were among the first provided for."

The charge regarding his family seems to have been exaggerated. While he did appoint 40 of his relatives, or relatives of Julia, to official posts, they were all of a minor nature. His brother-in-law, Frederick Dent, assumed many of the responsibilities that would today be performed by a private secretary. Dent received callers and booked the president's appointments, as well as conducting other business for Grant at the White House. Other relatives received appointments as customs officials, Indian traders, and local postmasters. The cabinet appointments were another matter. Elihu Washburne was selected to serve as secretary of state. Washburne was ill-suited to the position and was a most unlikely candidate, but he had been one of Grant's greatest supporters and was from his hometown of Galena. The fact is that Washburne did not want to be secretary of state. What he desired was to be appointed minister to France, but he felt that he would be more warmly received in that country if he went there as a former secretary of state. Washburne held the cabinet office for only a week before resigning the post, accepting his appointment as an ambassador, and taking his leave for Paris.

Alexander T. Stewart, of New York, was chosen to become secretary of the treasury. Stewart was a wealthy merchant who had acquired a personal fortune in business, and Grant felt that he could bring his financial genius to the government. What Grant failed to consider was the fact that there was a law on the books preventing any person engaged in mercantile pursuits from becoming head of the nation's finances. Grant then selected George S. Boutwell to fill the vacancy as treasury secretary. Boutwell hailed from Massachusetts and was an honest and upstanding man, but he had no experience, qualifications, or aptitude for financial affairs.

John A. Rawlins, Grant's old staff officer from Civil War days, was made secretary of war, despite the fact that he was suffering from advanced stages of tuberculosis. Rawlins's disease would cause him to be secretary of war in name only, and he would die later that same year. Though a few of Grant's appointments proved to be solid selections, the majority were of the nature described here, causing the seven cabinet positions to be occupied by 24 different men during the course of his term in office.

Even with the upheaval in his own cabinet, Grant's first term in office was relatively uneventful. Several years had now passed since the end of the war, and the nation was experiencing strong economic growth. Many people attributed these good times to Grant and his administration, causing his popularity to soar. The major political events to occur during his first term in office were the passage of the Fifteenth Amendment to the Constitution, the Amnesty Act, the Enforcement Act, and the Ku Klux Klan Act. The first provided for suffrage regardless of race, color, or previous condition of servitude, and the last gave the president authority to protect black rights. During this term, the military divisions of the former Confederacy reorganized state governments and sent representatives to Congress. The nation was prospering, and Reconstruction seemed to be reuniting the country. Indeed, Grant's only misstep during his first term seems to have been his pet project of annexing Santo Domingo, now known as the Dominican Republic, into the United States. The U.S. Navy had long wanted a base in the Caribbean, and Santo Domingo offered a suitable port for such operations. The country had just recently obtained its freedom from Spain, and its government favored joining with the United States. Grant was interested in obtaining a Caribbean port for the navy, but he had other reasons to support annexation. The majority of the population of Santo Domingo were blacks, and Grant felt that having the island as a state would offer an alternative to the former slaves in the South, providing them with a safe place to relocate to escape the discrimination and violence they were being subjected to. He also believed that this option to leave would place Southern blacks in a better position to negotiate labor issues with their white neighbors. Grant presented a treaty to annex Santo Domingo to Congress in 1870, but it failed to receive the support needed to turn it into law. Grant convinced enough senators to support a fact-finding expedition to the island. Three commissioners were sent to Santo Domingo, and upon their return, their report favored annexation. But the Senate would not be moved. The treaty was not brought to the floor for a vote, and the idea was allowed to die from inactivity.

The election of 1872 threatened to unseat the Republicans from power in much the same manner as the Democrats had been ousted in 1860. A split occurred in the party when liberal Republicans launched a concerted push to reform their party and politics in general. The liberal faction, led by men such as Horace Greeley, Francis Adams, and Carl Schurz, called a convention in May 1872 to be held at Cincinnati, Ohio. The attending delegates voted to break with the mainstream Republican Party and form a third-party alternative. They called for the immediate recall of all Federal soldiers then in the South, the elimination of political patronage, a return to the gold standard, a renewed emphasis on public education, and national expansion. Horace Greeley was elected as their nominee for president, with Gratz Brown chosen to be his running mate. This split in the Republican Party threatened to allow the Democrats to recover the White House while their political rivals bickered among themselves.

The Republicans held their convention in Philadelphia in June. Grant was renominated by acclamation, while Senator Henry Wilson was selected to replace Colfax as his running mate. The Republican Party was divided against itself, and all that was left to the Democrats was to nominate a candidate of sufficient national stature to pluck the presidency away from them. The only problem was that the Democratic Party had no such person to nominate. No candidate had the name recognition or public approval needed to undertake the campaign. In one of the strangest events ever to transpire in American political history, the Democratic Party decided to nominate the Greeley-Brown ticket to run for them and adopted the liberal Republican platform in its entirety. Greeley and his liberal associates agreed to accept the nomination because they believed that they could take over the Democratic Party and use it to defeat the political agenda of the radicals.

The election of 1872 witnessed only Republican candidates running for president. Grant represented the radical faction of the party, and Greeley, adopted by the Democrats, represented the views of the liberal faction. As he had done in 1868, Grant declined to campaign for himself. Greeley followed Seymour's precedent and set out on an ambitious speaking tour of the country, delivering 200 speeches in a matter of ten days. Greeley's words were upstaged by the antics of his running mate, Gratz Brown. Brown was drunk during his speech at Yale University, and he fainted from intoxication during a speech in New York City. Newspaper editors ignored Greeley's speeches and political views to focus on the disgraceful conduct of Brown, and the Republicans took advantage of the situation to engage in mud-slinging against their opponents. The campaign quickly deteriorated into one of the dirtiest in American history, causing Greeley to state, "I have been assailed so bitterly that I hardly knew whether I was running for the presidency or the penitentiary."

Republicans sought to improve their chances in the election through the use of the Reconstruction Enforcement Act. Federal officials in the South arrested any white accused of conspiring to keep blacks from voting. More than 1,000 such arrests were made in North Carolina alone, many of them in an attempt to discourage any Democratic opposition in the state. The Republican ticket was not popular among whites in the South, and it was therefore necessary to encourage as heavy of a black turnout as possible. In the end, the black vote in the South was sufficiently strong to swing those states in favor of Grant, who captured 286 of the 352 possible electoral votes. Grant even received 56 percent of the popular vote, the highest total since the election of 1828, when Andrew Jackson won the presidency. It would not be surpassed until 1904, when Teddy Roosevelt was swept into office on a wave of popularity. The campaign was taxing on both candidates. Greeley would die a few weeks after the election. Grant had been personally stung by the viciousness of the campaign, and he breathed a sigh of relief when it was over. "I have been the subject of abuse and slander, scarcely ever equaled in political history, which today I feel that I can afford to disregard, in view of your verdict, which I gratefully accept as my vindication."

Grant's second term as president proved to be far more eventful than his first. Scandal rocked his second four years, and his administration seemed to be mired in graft and corruption. In 1869, there was a gold speculation scheme that threatened to severely damage the nation's economy. Grant's own brother-in-law had been a coconspirator in the scheme, and at least one member of his administration had taken bribes from the speculators. Grant, however, seems to have been totally innocent of any wrongdoing in the affair, and he was responsible

for thwarting the scheme by ordering the treasury to release millions
of dollars in gold to the public. Most people gave Grant the benefit of
the doubt in this scandal, but in his second term, the scandals came so
frequently that the public coined the term "Grantism" to describe the
corruption in his administration. There was a scandal involving mis-
appropriated government funds connected with the transcontinental
railroad. There was a furor over graft and corruption at the New York
Custom House. The postal service was found guilty of accepting bribes
to award lucrative postal delivery contracts in the South and along
the Pacific coast. In 1873, the Salary Grab took place, in which Congress secretly passed a bill that doubled the salary of the president
and increased their own pay by 50 percent. In 1874, the secretary of
the treasury, William Richardson, contracted with John Sanborn to
collect money owed to the Internal Revenue Service. Treasury department officials were pressured not to collect outstanding debts in order
to allow Sanborn time to do so himself. Of the $420,000 Sanborn col-
lected, $213,000 was paid to him as a commission. A great deal of
this money was paid to unnamed associates and listed as expenses by
Sanborn. Though most people felt that Secretary Richardson was one
of these associates, no paper trail could be found to charge him. In 1875,
Secretary of the Interior Columbus Delano was found to have taken
bribes to secure fraudulent land grants. Delano's son, John, and Orvil
Grant, the president's brother, had both been given lucrative carto-
graphical contracts, even though neither man was a qualified surveyor
or had performed any surveying work. Grant's attorney general was
caught accepting bribes not to prosecute cases. He was also using jus-
tice department funds to pay for his personal living expenses. In 1875,
Grant's new secretary of the treasury, Benjamin Bristow, uncovered
a conspiracy within the Internal Revenue Service in which whiskey
distillers in several states evaded paying federal excise tax by making payoffs to government agents. Both of Grant's private secretar-
ies, Horace Porter and Orville Babcock, would be indicted for having
taken payoffs in the scheme. Grant appointed a special prosecutor to
handle the trials of the Whiskey Ring conspirators, but when that
prosecutor accused the president of hampering the investigations,
Grant promptly replaced him with another lawyer. No sooner was the
Whiskey Ring scandal ended than it was discovered that Secretary of

War William Belknap had been taking bribes to award government contracts for trading posts on Indian reservations. Grant allowed Belknap to resign his office rather than face impeachment by the Senate. The Department of the Navy was not immune to the scandals either. Undersecretary George Robeson was accused of taking large payoffs from a government contractor and was suspected of embezzling $15 million that could not be accounted for in the navy's budget.

By all accounts, Grant was innocent of any connection with the graft and corruption taking place within his administration. An examination of his financial records shows that he did not receive any of the huge sums of money associated with these schemes. Though he was accused of corruption in several instances, he was found innocent of all charges. The verdict of history is only able to convict him of showing a glaring lack of judgment in surrounding himself with unscrupulous and conniving men. His own honesty aside, he was guilty of failing to protect the public trust from the outrages committed by his own political family.

One would think that the number and severity of the scandals that rocked his second term in office would surely have influenced Grant to retire from public life as soon as he could. Such was not the case. In 1875, he made known his ambition to seek a third term, and he seemed to be the front-runner for the Republican nomination in 1876. But the Democrats had won a majority in Congress in the 1874 elections, and they voted a resolution to uphold the tradition of a two-term limit on the presidency. Grant then withdrew his name from consideration.

At the conclusion of his presidency, Grant planned to take a long and leisurely tour of the world. He had never held much regard for politics, and now, following eight years as the nation's top politician, he was thoroughly disgusted with the entire process. On May 17, 1877, Grant, Julia, and their son Jesse set out from Philadelphia harbor for Europe. Their first stop was England, where Grant received a hero's welcome as an ex-president and the greatest general in the world. Grant and his family zigzagged across Europe before making a stop in the Holy Land. They traveled to India, China, Siam, and Japan. Everywhere he went, he was greeted by heads of state and crowds of citizens who huddled together to catch a glimpse of the famous general who had won the Civil War. The trip took more than two years to complete, and the Grants did not return to America until September 1879.

After a few months at home, Grant took a trip to Cuba and Mexico in hopes of establishing business connections there. His financial resources were beginning to run low, and some means to replenish them needed to be found. In the back of his mind, Grant thought that being elected president again just might be the solution. He made known his desire to serve a third term and pointed out that the two-term limitation was a custom and not a law. When the Republican Party held its national convention in 1880, Grant received 304 votes on the first ballot cast. A total of 378 were needed to secure the nomination. His chief rivals were Elihu Washburne and John Sherman. By the time a third ballot was taken, a Pennsylvania delegate cast a single vote for James A. Garfield. Ballot followed ballot, as none of the nominees could garner the total number of votes necessary to secure the nomination. By the time the 14th ballot was taken, 16 delegates changed their votes and joined with the delegate from Pennsylvania in supporting Garfield. Each successive ballot saw the votes for Garfield increasing, and by the time the 36th vote was taken, 382 delegates had shifted their support from Washburne and Sherman to join the Garfield camp. On the final ballot, Grant still had 304 delegates pledged to his candidacy. Much chagrined by the loss, Grant accused his supporters of dishonesty, stating, "They should not have placed me in nomination unless they felt perfectly sure of my success."

The foiled hopes for another term as president left Grant still searching for a source of income for himself and his family. Though he had $100,000 in personal assets, he felt that the income they generated was not sufficient to support their needs. The income would have allowed him to live comfortably in Galena, but Grant desired to live in New York, and he would need to make more money to do so. In 1881, he made another business trip to Mexico, which eventually resulted in him being elected president of the Mexican Southern Railroad. His compensation for this position has never been disclosed, but Grant spent a portion of every workday at Wall Street, going over paperwork and signing contracts for the firm.

In the late 1870s, Grant's son Ulysses Jr. made the acquaintance of Ferdinand Ward, a self-proclaimed financial wizard. Ward convinced the younger Grant that he should invest his money in a joint business venture, and the two men opened Grant & Ward, a banking and brokerage house. Ulysses Jr. invested $100,000 in the firm, and his father, still looking for a source of income, put in $100,000 of his own money. Ward was a sham artist. The firm never had any real assets and never conducted any real business. The affiliation of the Grants allowed him to use the Grant name to bilk other investors out of huge sums of money. He would approach men of substance seeking capital to finance bogus government contracts, which he said he learned about through General Grant. Ward got the Marine National Bank involved in his scheme, and by the time bank president James Fish knew what was going on, he was so deeply entangled that he became a conspirator with Ward. By paying dividends to investors with money stolen from new clients, Ward was able to keep his swindling act going for three years. Grant ended up putting all of his money on account with Grant & Ward, and many of his friends and relatives did the same. Fake bonds and stock certificates were given for these investments, and by 1884, Grant thought that he was a very rich man with assets totaling almost $2.5 million. In May 1884, a depositor withdrew a large sum of money from the Marine National Bank, leaving it short on funds. Fish had been underwriting Ward's fraudulent activities for some time now, and the assets he claimed to have in the bank were as fictitious as the bonds and stocks that were being given to the investors. The scheme was about to come undone, and Ward knew it. He went to Grant to tell him of a temporary setback with the bank and to see if the general could raise $150,000 for a short-term loan to insure their investments. Grant paid a call to William Vanderbilt and asked to borrow the money. Vanderbilt told him that he had no faith in Ward or in the firm of Grant & Ward. He would lend no money to them. But he would make a personal loan to Grant. Grant gave Ward the check from Vanderbilt, which he promptly cashed and kept for himself. The bank was folding and Ward knew it. The firm of Grant & Ward had little more than $67,000 in assets to cover liabilities of almost $17 million. The bank went under, the true status of Grant & Ward became public knowledge, and Grant was personally and financially destroyed. The family did not even have money to buy food or other daily necessities. Two benefactors sent the Grants checks totaling $2,000, and that is the money they lived on for a considerable time.

Century Magazine had previously approached Grant to ask him to write three articles about the war. They offered $500 for each article. Initially, Grant had told them that he was not interested in writing the pieces, as he was trying to forget the war. After the loss of all his money, however, Grant had a change of heart. Grant wrote the articles, and when they appeared in the magazine, distribution jumped markedly, to the point that Century paid him a $1,500 bonus. In the meantime, Century had entered into talks with Grant concerning the writing of his memoirs. The company wished to publish the book, but they would give the general no advance for writing it. Instead, they offered a standard 10 percent royalty on the copies sold. Samuel Clemens, better known as the writer Mark Twain, was the principal owner in the publishing firm of Charles L. Webster and Company. He learned of the proposed book and decided to try to get it for his own publishing house. Twain was familiar with Grant, so he stopped by the general's house for an informal meeting. He told Grant that Century was taking advantage of him and offered to give the general a $25,000 advance and a 20 percent royalty on all books sold. Twain told Grant to see if Century would match his offer, and if so, he could make up his mind from there. Century declined to offer any advance and stated that they could go no higher than 10 percent for the royalty. Grant therefore decided to sign with Twain.

The contract for his memoirs provided Grant with a means to financially provide for his family, and he set to work with the same focused determination that had characterized all actions in his life. At first, he dictated his accounts to a stenographer, but he was finding it increasingly hard to speak. A nagging pain in his throat was diagnosed as cancer, and his voice would soon be gone. After two months, he found it so hard to speak that the stenographer was dismissed, and he began writing the memoirs longhand on large sheets of paper. Day after day, he would sit in a chair—knit cap on his head, bundles of blankets covering his now frail body—putting words to paper in an effort to finish the work before death came for him. Many days he was too sick to be out of bed, but he plodded onward with a grim resolution to see the thing done. The general's condition and the advancement of the disease

Pen in hand, the old warrior struggles to complete his memoirs before cancer claims his life. Grant would win his last battle, completing his manuscript a week before his death, and the publication of his memoirs would provide a much needed source of income for his family. (U.S. Army Military History Institute)

were reported regularly in the newspapers, and the nation joined in collective hope that the old warrior would win this last battle. Grant's resolve was tenacious. It was as if he clung to life by sheer will alone. Month after month, he endured the mind-numbing pain as he wrote down the memories of his military career. By the middle of July 1885, he was putting the final touches on the manuscript, and the memoirs were complete. Grant would not live to see them published. He died at his home in Mount McGregor, New York, on July 23, 1885, at the age of 63. He had indeed won his last battle. His memoirs proved to be one of the greatest commercial publishing successes of the era, selling over 300,000 copies. Proceeds from the sale, amounting to more than $450,000, were turned over to the estate to benefit his widow. His final act had provided the financial security for his family that Grant had spent his entire life trying to attain.

Grant's body was placed on a funeral train in Albany, New York. When the train passed by West Point, the entire cadet body of the

U.S. Military Academy turned out to salute the fallen hero. The train continued on to New York City, where his body was laid to rest in a funeral attended by throngs of dignitaries, family, friends, former comrades, and saddened countrymen. The City of New York raised money to construct a tomb for the general, and on April 27, 1897, the 75th anniversary of his birth, his body was transferred to it. Grant's Tomb is the largest mausoleum in North America and serves not only as the final resting place for him and his wife, Julia; it is also a monument to the man who led the nation's armies to the end of the Civil War and served two terms as president. In 1902, Congress commissioned a memorial to be built to Grant at the foot of Capitol Hill. It was the largest expenditure of money the government had made for a monument up to that time. The work would take 20 years to complete and would be dedicated in 1922. The bronze equestrian statue of Grant would stand more than 17 feet tall and would be placed atop a 22-foot marble pedestal. He would look down on Washington for eternity as a larger-than-life figure, much the same way that most of his countrymen had viewed him during his lifetime.

AFTERWORD

The life of Ulysses S. Grant is an unending story of failure and redemption. It is the story of a common man called to do great things, a man possessed of few latent talents or abilities who made up for natural deficiencies through grit and determination. As such, it is a celebration of the human spirit, a reminder that we are all capable of achieving great things if we tenaciously hold to our dreams and are willing to invest the effort and sacrifice to make them come true. It is also the story of perseverance. The numerous failures and tragedies that rocked Grant's life did not cause him to give up the fight or surrender his ambitions. In fact, he could be the spokesman for the old saying, "That which does not break you only serves to make you stronger." Grant was never broken. He struggled through adversity with the heart of a warrior, his eye always firmly planted on the prize.

Grant's approach to all things was simple and pragmatic. He had a mechanical mind that could see things only as they were and could not contemplate theory or abstract thoughts. The application of simple logic was the basis for all of his military campaigns during the Civil War. A man who met him for the first time during the war described Grant as a man who had determined to ram his head through a brick wall and was just about to do it. His campaigns were built on the same sort of straightforward, no-nonsense determination to seek out the enemy and defeat him at any cost. Grant has been condemned by many critics for the excessive casualties his armies sustained in conducting their campaigns, and some of the arguments are certainly justified, but no one can argue with the results. He captured Vicksburg and opened the Mississippi River. He was the commanding officer at Chattanooga when the siege was lifted and the Confederate army defeated, even if he actually had little to do with the operation. He clamped on to Lee's Army of Northern Virginia like a bulldog and refused to allow it to breathe until the life was finally choked out of it. From Fort Henry to Appomattox Court House, his name became synonymous with victory, regardless of the cost, and by the end of the war he had become the symbol of Federal military strength.

Grant's presidency was a comic opera of scandal and corruption. The eight years of his administration are known to history as one of the darkest times in American politics. But Grant emerges from this period as an honest, though naive, man, whose greatest fault seems to have been in surrounding himself with men of questionable character and scruples. If any guilt is to be found, it is that he was somehow able to remain so completely ignorant of the conspiracies taking place all around him. His simple, mechanical mind could not conceive of such schemes, and he was not perceptive enough to discover that talent in others. He was, at core, a farmer and a soldier and was wholly unsuited for life in the political arena. This fact was lost on him, as any philosophical thought might have been, and he sought to be elected to the presidency for a third term on two different occasions.

Grant's handling of his personal finances was the greatest failure of his life. He had always desired to live a comfortable existence. His early days at Hardscrabble, when he delivered wood door-to-door to earn money, had left a marked impression on him. Grant feared poverty. He had seen what becomes of destitute men and had been humiliated by working as a clerk in his brother's tannery. He wanted to make sure that he never had to scratch out a living or beg for a job again. Though he had acquired huge sums of money during his life, he was always looking to increase his worth and to expand his fortunes, and his efforts invariably led to the loss of the assets he had started with. He began the final chapter of his life as destitute as he had been when he accepted his brother's handout back in Galena and was dependant on the charity of strangers for his daily bread. Fierce pride and unflinching determination carried him through his final battle and enabled him to accomplish in death what he had never been able to do in life: provide a long-term income for his family. It is appropriate that his likeness adorns our national currency, for he spent a great part of his life trying to amass money.

Ulysses S. Grant remains today one of the nation's foremost military heroes. His campaigns have been written about for almost 150 years, and he has been the focus of numerous biographies. His legend is not diminished by the failures in his life; it is intensified by the substance those failures lend to his story. I think we celebrate the man because we all see a little of ourselves within him. Fraught with the same faults and frailties that most of us are susceptible to, he still achieved great things, which many of us aspire to do. He was one of us, a common man who soared to great heights, and isn't that what we all dream of?

BIBLIOGRAPHICAL ESSAY

A wealth of information has been written concerning the life of Ulysses S. Grant. As is true with most great men, many of the biographies available are little more than eulogies or tributes, praising his achievements while overlooking his failures. Fortunately, there are a number of good, solid biographies written by true historians that cut away the adulation and examine Grant's life in great detail. This book has been compiled through the use of several such works. First and foremost, I have relied on Grant's own words to tell the story of his life. *Personal Memoirs of U. S. Grant*, the book he completed just before his death, has provided personal explanations for his actions, as well as insight into his thoughts and feelings. *Campaigning with Grant* by Horace Porter and *Military History of Ulysses S. Grant: From April, 1861 to April, 1865* by Adam Badeau were both written by officers who served on Grant's staff. They are valuable resources in terms of providing a glimpse of how the general's subordinates viewed him, as well as an inside look at the workings of Grant's military family. Both books tend to be more partisan than objective in nature, however, and historical incidents that might not reflect well on the general are many times glossed over or not mentioned at all. Of the more recent biographies,

Meet General Grant, by W. E. Woodward, is a staple. Woodward presents an objective analysis of Grant, with a fair and balanced evaluation of his accomplishments and failures. He also brings a great deal of historical context into this biography by giving the reader a firm grasp on events transpiring in other places and how they affected Grant's actions. *Grant: A Biography,* by William S. McFeely, is another of the more recent biographies that strips away the adulation and examines Grant the man, instead of Grant the legend. McFeely's research is commendable, and his interpretations of motives and actions in various stages of his life show that he is an expert on the subject, as well as an outstanding biographer.

Other books of interest for the person wishing to learn more about Grant's life would include *Grant Moves South* by Bruce Catton, *Let Us Have Peace* by Howard N. Meyer, *Grant and Sherman: The Friendship That Won the Civil War* by Charles Bracelen Flood, *Grant and His Generals* by Clarence Edward Macartney, *The Battle of Belmont: Grant Strikes South* by Nathaniel Cheairs Hughes Jr., *Grant Wins the War: Decision at Vicksburg* by James R. Arnold, and *The Training Ground: Grant, Lee, Sherman and Davis in the Mexican American War, 1846–1848* by Martin Dugard. All of these books give highly detailed descriptions of Grant's actions in various campaigns and offer more in-depth information about certain stages of his life than can be included in any one-volume biography. *Century Magazine*'s compilation of contemporary articles that became the four-volume set titled *Battles and Leaders* is not devoted to Grant, but many of the articles it contains deal with Grant and his campaigns and were written by his contemporaries.

Information on Grant can be found in abundance on the Internet, from the official website of the White House to Ulyssesgrant.org, a site dedicated to preserving the memory and legacy of the general. Typing his name into a search engine will result in a wealth of sites that cover every aspect of his life, and one will find both supporters and detractors in abundance. A basic knowledge of the war, and of Grant's life, is necessary to cut through the bias, pro and con, that can be found in the various blog spots and open forums that go beyond the standard biographical essays.

INDEX

About the Author

ROBERT P. BROADWATER is the author of *Gettysburg as the Generals Remembered It: Postwar Perspectives of Ten Commanders* and *American Generals of the Revolutionary War: A Biographical Dictionary*. He has written or contributed to 30 books on the American Revolution and the Civil War. He has also had more than 100 articles published on military history, covering the periods of the French and Indian War through World War II. Broadwater resides in Bellwood, Pennsylvania.